Native Landscaping
for Wildlife
and People

Missouri Department of Conservation
P.O. Box 180
Jefferson City, MO 65102-0180

Acknowledgments

I sincerely appreciate the generous support and contributions from many knowledgeable and giving people. I thank them for sharing their information, experiences, talents and, most of all, their time to produce this book. I hope you are pleased with the results.

Although I have dreamed about writing this book for many years, it came alive with the Grow Native! program of the Missouri Department of Conservation, which was created and developed by Cheryl Riley, Judy Allmon and many others who are committed to native landscaping. Thanks for helping make this book a reality.

Don Kurz of the Missouri Department of Conservation and Craig Tufts of the National Wildlife Federation were the principal scientific reviewers of all texts and tables. I am very grateful to them for the untold hours they spent reading, re-reading and making many valuable suggestions along the way.

Many chapters and tables were also reviewed by botanists, horticulturists, arborists, urban biologists, herpetologists, entomologists and wildlife biologists from both the public and private sectors. Mervin Wallace, Scott Woodbury, Tim Smith, George Yatskievych, Richard Heitzman, Joe Werner, Mike Arduser, John Kabrick, Jeff Briggler, Bill McGuire and Wayne Wittmeyer all made significant contributions to this project. I also thank Jim Rathert and Cliff White for contributing photographs.

Charlotte Overby, Paula Kapfer and Martha Daniels deserve much credit for the many hours spent editing, organizing and designing the manuscript and detailed tables.

I am most grateful to my partner and wife, Karen, who not only made my initial words logical and understandable with her editing, but most important, listened to my ideas and skillfully gave me criticism when I asked for it. Her patience and understanding were beyond belief.

DAVE TYLKA

3

Native Landscaping
for Wildlife
and People

Jim Rathert

How to Use Native Midwestern
Plants to Beautify Your Property
and Benefit Wildlife

by DAVE TYLKA

Published by the Missouri
Department of Conservation

Table of Contents

Introduction

After a quick greeting and handshake at the door, our friend Lyle grabs the binoculars off the counter and makes a beeline to the corner of our kitchen table where he positions himself to watch the activities at the birdfeeder. He watches the goldfinches and humming-birds, yet stays within earshot of conversation.

Lyle, like millions of Americans, loves to watch wildlife around the home. Our family and thousands of others throughout the Midwest enjoy attracting wildlife to the yard with birdfeeders, butterfly and hummingbird gardens and bat houses.

But by far the single most compelling reason why wildlife species visit our place is that we almost exclu-sively landscape with native plants. Our small patch of prairie, the woodland wildflowers and trees, and the various shrubs between these two communities furnish food and cover for both open grassland wildlife and forest-dwelling animals.

Our sun and shade landscapes connect us to nature. The diverse array of native plants and animals improves our quality of life by offering excitement, change, the challenge of uncovering the unknown, peace and a warm feeling that comes from caring for the land. I can still remember the first time we awoke to the laughing of barred owls outside our bedroom window. Our hearts did race that night.

Watching the parade of change across the native landscapes is intoxicating, especially within the forest as the flowers magically ascend from the forest floor up through the canopy. First come the flowering blood-roots and other wildflowers, next the spicebush, service-berry, redbud and flowering dogwood, and then the oak and hickory catkins. At the end of the growing season, acorns and fall colors serve as the finale.

Pat Whalen

Our family and friends have spent many memorable moments together trying to identify the bird, blossom or bizarre-looking beetle that we discovered perched on the top of a coneflower. Many natural mysteries are never solved, but that's part of the magnetism that draws us outside and away from the television.

Often, when I get home after a long day in the classroom, I quickly throw my homework inside the house and escape to the refuge of the yard. A slow journey among the prairie wildflowers and the forest trees calms my soul and renews my spirit. Surrounding myself with nature helps put things in perspective. As we humans continue to over-consume, pollute and modify the landscape to make room for more people, our property gives a small piece of habitat back to native plants and animals. From a natural perspective, there are few endeavors around the home that are more rewarding than native landscaping.

I hope this book helps you, too, find the same excitement, wonder and peace with your surrounding native landscape. If you follow the chapter-by-chapter progression in the book, you are well on your way to attracting and enjoying wildlife around your home.

The first three chapters introduce you to important natural concepts and the basics of making plans and designs. Chapters four and five lead you step-by-step to develop shade- and sun-dominated landscapes. The next chapter suggests how you can attract specific wildlife groups, such as birds and butterflies, to your yard. Chapter seven focuses on small habitats, such as pools, marshes and glades, while Chapter eight broadens your options and explains a whole range of ideas that can be implemented on larger properties. The last chapter provides tips on how you can attract wildlife closer to your house so you and your family can observe them more easily. I wish you success.

PAGE 6 *A Question Mark butterfly enhances the dramatic, spherical form of a buttonbush, one of the best shrub nectar sources for butterflies and many other insects.* **LEFT AND ABOVE** *Purple coneflowers and yellow Missouri coneflowers add grace to any summer garden, and are also favorite food sources for butterflies. These are just a few of the more than 3,000 Midwestern native plants that could beautify your property and benefit wildlife.*

seeing the big picture

Chapter One

The heart of the Midwest is blessed with a wonderful array of plants and animals found in landscapes of oak-hickory forests and flowing tall grass prairies. Public conservation areas, parks and natural areas are but an easy drive for most people. Perhaps you and others who share your passion for nature have discovered bright orange box turtles searching for food among the spring wildflower carpet or the yellow and black flash of a meadowlark in a sea of purple prairie coneflowers.

Have you ever wished you could bottle up these experiences and set them free around your home to enjoy throughout the year? By gathering information, doing a little planning and investing some time, labor and money for materials, you can gradually transform your yard into a wildlife haven.

Benefits Beyond Your Property Lines

Landscaping for wildlife adds color, diversity and spice to life. Unlike manicured lawns, the natural beauty of native grasses, wildflowers, shrubs and trees offers variety and attracts wildlife. Nature also fascinates the mind and lifts the spirit. Our quality of life is enhanced by bright red cardinals, yellow sulphur butterflies and bluejays. For many of us, the most fun is in seeing and studying the unknown. Why do some birds eat seeds, others prefer berries, while still others perch and swoop down on flying insects?

Furnish wildlife with a landscape of food, water and cover and the windows of your home become windows to the natural world. Native vegetation will change throughout the seasons and, in turn, furnish you with a kaleidoscope of form and color. Some amazing mysteries of nature will unfold within view.

Your home is like a photographer's blind. You can see out while wildlife cannot see in very well. Make it a habit to have binoculars, field guides and a camera close at hand to enjoy your wildlife guests and expand your mind. If you have paperwork to do, a book to read or

Jim Rathert

Jim Rathert

CHAPTER COVER PAGE *Wetlands are just one of the habitat types found in the Midwest. Forests, prairies, glades and savannas are common throughout the region.* **ABOVE, BOTTOM** *There are almost 2,000 species of sulphur butterflies in the world and many—like this dogface sulphur butterfly at rest on a purple coneflower—inhabit the Midwest.* **ABOVE, TOP** *This mockingbird—a juvenile as evidenced by its speckled breast— has found a perch in an American beauty berry.*

13

Jim Rathert

Dave Tylka

other sit-down tasks, do them in front of a window where you can look out periodically. Better yet, take it outside to a vantage point where you can appreciate your landscaping. Most people spend more time at home than in any other place. If you want to brighten your life, naturalize your property. You'll bring joy and excitement to your address.

By landscaping for wildlife, you are in essence restoring some of the natural qualities to the land, especially if you use only native plants (see Chapter Two). Unfortunately, most of the prairies and old-growth forests in the Midwest have been converted into agricultural and developed landscapes. Croplands and manicured lawns are not very appealing to most species of native wildlife. By converting energy-consuming lawns back into more diverse natural communities, you are contributing not only to a more environmentally sound landscape but also furnishing food and cover for birds, butterflies and mammals.

Besides the benefits to wildlife, planting trees and shrubs around your yard reduces your energy bills and increases the value of your property. If you locate evergreen trees on the north and west sides of your home, you save on heating costs because these plants help block your house from cold winter winds. In the summer, deciduous trees and shrubs that grow on the south side of your home provide shade to help reduce cooling costs. Research shows that planting shrubs and trees increases property market values, which is important if you ever choose to move.

Many suburban and urban dwellers have lost connection to their natural resources and, at best, experience nature via the television. Turn off the television and tune into your property. Natural landscapes offer first-hand outdoor experiences, as well as a lesson or two about the environment. Feed your curiosity, dirty

ABOVE, TOP *In the fall, watch closely for walkingsticks. These harmless insects are masters of camouflage.* **ABOVE, BOTTOM** *Praying mantises are highly beneficial because they are voracious predators of insects, although this one was found devouring a five-lined skink.* **RIGHT** *Blazing star, also called gayfeather, is common in prairies and rocky, open ground. They do well as cut flowers in a vase and also dry nicely for use in dried-flower arrangements.*

your knees and take a close look at the action around your flowers. Discover the predator-prey dramas that unfold before your eyes when insects drop in for a meal of flower nectar and instead become dinner for praying mantises and crab spiders that wait in ambush. Instead of afternoon soap operas, watch and listen as male ruby-throated hummingbirds zoom up and down in their J-shaped courtship flight. These are true-to-life bird dating and mating behaviors. Sharing these outdoor experiences with others around the home strengthens friendships, family bonds and fuels conversations for years to come.

Location, Location, Location

The most important factor, by far, that affects the success of attracting wildlife to your yard is location. The closer you live to a natural community, such as a forest, prairie or wetland, the greater your chances are for getting a variety of wildlife species to visit. If you are surrounded by miles of concrete, asphalt or agricultural fields, only the most mobile and adaptable wildlife may be lured to your backyard oasis. People who live in rural towns among corn and soybean fields probably won't be able to attract as much wildlife as suburbanites who live close to urban creeks or patches of urban woods. No matter where you live, birds, butterflies, bats and other flying animals can be enticed to your yard with the right habitat.

However, the farther you live away from natural communities, the harder it is for wildlife to find you, except maybe during migration. Midwesterners who live miles from natural communities report migrating hummingbirds at their feeders during March and April or August and September, but never see hummingbirds during the summer breeding season, which is typically May through July. If you live within walking distance of a forest, prairie or wetland community, or if you are close to a wooded creek or unmowed railroad track corridor that ties you to one of those communities, furnishing a connection from your property to those habitats may be very rewarding.

Jim Rathert

To welcome dispersing,

migrating or feeding

wildlife into your

yard, your property

must be accessible

to them.

Dave Tylka

Habitat Corridors—the Wildlife Connection

All wildlife species move about. As many animals successfully breed and produce young, the original habitat may not have enough food and cover to support both the parents and offspring. Often at the encouragement of the parents, young animals leave home to seek new habitat and stake out their own territories. Young males may travel long distances to stake out a new territory and produce their own young. If you somehow connect your property directly or indirectly to larger blocks of wildlife habitat—create a wildlife corridor—then dispersing animals may wander in your direction.

Many of us are familiar with the seasonal migrations of the orange- and black-colored monarch butterflies and the colorful neotropical songbirds that fly thousands of miles to Central and South America when the weather turns cold. But some of us do not realize that most walking or crawling, non-flying wildlife species also make seasonal migrations. Although not as dramatic as the elk and caribou migrations that we see on television, amphibians, reptiles and mammals of the Midwest also move to different habitats to feed or reproduce.

Most prairie and forest species of amphibians return each spring or fall to temporary pools, ponds and other wetland areas to reproduce. Prairie inhabitants, such as the plains leopard frog, tiger salamander and northern crayfish frog, seek water to breed. Forest-dwellers, such as spotted and ringed salamanders and the gray treefrog, migrate to water to breed and lay eggs.

When seasonal foods are depleted in one habitat, the plant-eating herbivores such as squirrels leave one feeding area for another. Many carnivores—or meat-eating species—such as garter snakes and southern leopard frogs visit distant habitats searching for prey. During the summer months, leopard frogs travel far from water into grasslands and forests looking for insects to eat. Red and gray foxes, raccoons and other wildlife that eat either plants or animals—omnivores—may travel many miles each night searching for food.

To welcome dispersing, migrating or feeding wildlife into your yard, your property must be accessible to them. Vegetated wildlife corridors provide this connection. Although some large, mobile wildlife species such as deer can travel long distances over a variety of habitats to find food, most other wild animals require vegetated corridors or "green space" as travel lanes. A diversity of grasses, wildflowers, shrubs and trees in these corridors furnishes cover for wildlife on the move.

If your yard backs up to a stream, forest, prairie or unmowed railroad corridor, you have a connection. If your yard and neighborhood lack vegetated corridors, get connected. One of the simplest ways to develop a corridor is for you and members of your subdivision's leadership to adopt a no-mowing policy along a creek or linear strip of common ground that connects wildlife habitats to your neighborhood. Progressive developers preserve fingers of vegetation along ravines and creeks before construction. These vegetated corridors not only benefit wildlife, but also reduce soil erosion and storm water runoff. If you are a member of a conservation group or part of a local government, consider expanding this corridor concept to benefit your community.

Busy roads, especially around urban areas, seriously limit wildlife movement. Multi-lane and high-speed highways are tremendous barriers to box turtles and other non-flying ground animals. Nationally, millions of reptiles and mammals die each year attempting to cross roads. Progressive highway departments are beginning to construct wildlife underpasses where busy roads cut through prime wildlife habitat. These underpasses allow animals safe passage and reduce wildlife and vehicle collisions. If you live close to a

Cliff White

LEFT *Landscaping with native plants often opens the door to other outdoor interests. Many people become hooked on birdwatching, keeping a seasonal journal or capturing wildlife—like this marbled salamander— on film.* **ABOVE** *In urban or heavily developed suburban areas, wildlife corridors can be hard to find. This one is small but consists of a strip of woods buffering a stream. It provides some cover and travel routes for birds and small mammals.*

Dave Tylka

Jim Rathert

highway, locate any existing underpasses or drainage culverts that animals may use and establish a vegetated connection from that underpass to your yard. If you live in a developing part of the community where large roads are being planned, contact the planners and encourage them to consider opportunities to build wildlife underpasses.

Wildlife Needs Habitat

Key landscape features that attract wildlife to your yard and then encourage them to stay around long enough for you to watch are referred to collectively as wildlife habitat. Habitat is defined as the appropriate food, water and cover that an animal needs to live and reproduce. Some wildlife species are generalists in their habitat needs while others are highly specialized.

If you ask people what types of wildlife they enjoy watching, some will say all kinds, others like birds, and many prefer butterflies. When selecting wildlife habitat plants for your yard, you may want to offer a whole smorgasbord of shade plants (see Chapter Four) or sun plants (see Chapter Five) to attract an assortment of animals. Different species of plants furnish food in different forms, such as leaves, seeds, berries, nuts and flower nectars or pollens. Or, to attract hummingbirds and butterflies, you may want to key into nectar-producing plants (see Chapter Six). Generally, the greater variety of vegetation you make available—grasses, wildflowers, shrubs and trees—the greater your chances are for attracting a larger diversity of wildlife.

ABOVE, TOP *Three-toed box turtles are found in woodland and brushy habitats. During the breeding season, male box turtles develop bright orange coloration on their heads.* **ABOVE, BOTTOM** *Blue jays are common year-round. They are related to crows and ravens and feed mainly on seeds and nuts.* **RIGHT** *Bluebells, sometimes called Virginia cowslip, are large, showy plants that grow up to two feet tall, often in large groups. They grow in moist, wooded areas.*

Strive for Biodiversity

As you increase the biodiversity or number of different species of plants and animals on your property, you also are enhancing the natural systems and improving the environmental health of your property. When you plant new species, you offer new food sources for more kinds of wildlife and even more food chains open up in your yard. Herbivores and omnivores attract carnivores such as praying mantises, lizards, toads and warblers. Daddy-long-legs are scavengers that eat organisms when they die. Fungi break down the decaying plants and animals and return nutrients back to the soil where they are taken up by plant roots. Natural materials are continually recycled.

As you increase biodiversity, you improve the health of your ecosystem. An ecosystem is a group of interdependent organisms that interact with each other and their physical environment. In healthy ecosystems, there are various checks and controls. For example, if caterpillar populations begin to get out of control, the predators, such as warblers and lizards, among others, help keep the population in check.

Wildlife—the Generalists and Specialists

Many animal species are versatile in their habitat requirements and are very adaptable, while others are more particular about their habitat and are more specialized. Offering habitat for highly adaptable species or generalists, such as bluejays, is easier than providing habitat for specialists, such as pileated woodpeckers.

Jim Rathert

Jim Rathert

Bluejays can feed on a wide array of plants and animals. To survive the winter, they bury acorns from a variety of oaks in the ground. Bluejays can nest in trees, shrubs or vines. Their nests are found in many different locations—urban, suburban and rural environments. Their nesting materials vary from twigs, bark, grass, lichens and moss to string, rags and paper.

Pileated woodpeckers, on the other hand, live in only mature forests and require large territories. Because of their large size—they are similar in size to crows—these birds need dead trees at least 12 inches in diameter to chisel out a home. The wood in the standing, dead trees—also called snags—must have some decay, yet be solid, not spongy. The size of the forest also influences the occurrence of pileated woodpeckers. Their territories range from 160 to 250 acres in size.

Pileated woodpeckers are rarely seen in forests without their main food source, carpenter ants. These large, black ants are important to mature forests because they help recycle dead and decaying wood. A forest without old or mature trees does not support carpenter ants and, therefore, does not provide habitat for specialists such as pileated woodpeckers.

Not all wildlife species fit nicely into categories. Some animals are generalists at one stage or time of their lives, while specialists during others. For example, adult butterflies are generalists when it comes to flower nectars but are selective when it comes to choosing a plant species for egg-laying and as food for their hatching caterpillars. Three-toed box turtles tend to be carnivorous when they are young and become more herbivorous as they grow older.

Jim Rathert

These examples should help you keep perspective as you work to attract wildlife. Be realistic in your expectations. Expect generalists and cherish specialists.

Sun and Shade Landscapes

Regardless of whether they are generalists or specialists, many wildlife species prefer one type of habitat over another. Three-toed box turtles are more commonly found in forests, while ornate box turtles typically inhabit open habitats, such as prairies and meadows. Chickadees and tufted titmice are forest birds that feed high in tree branches. Meadowlarks and dickcissels, in contrast, prefer open habitats, such as prairies and meadows, and feed among the grasses and wildflowers.

Although some generalist wildlife species use both sun and shade habitats, you probably will probably have the most success as you begin if you replicate the dominant type of habitat generally found in your vicinity. Don't overwhelm yourself with details about the many natural communities and their interrelationships. Instead, you can simplify the land communities of our region into two basic categories—shaded landscapes or forest communities dominated by trees, and sun landscapes or prairie communities dominated by grasses, flowers and shrubs. Read on for ways to develop these two basic landscapes in your own backyard and to learn what species of wildlife they attract.

LEFT *Pileated woodpeckers require many acres of mature forest habitat with several dead trees. Carpenter ants that live in the dead trees are an important source of food for pileated woodpeckers.* **ABOVE** *Cardinals, on the other hand, are generalists. They have adapted to rural and urban conditions and can successfully raise young in close proximity to people.*

favor the natives

Chapter Two

*W*hen choosing plants, one of the most important decisions that any home landscaper can make is how much emphasis to place on planting native plants, as opposed to exotic plants. All of the plants recommended in this book are native to the central, lower Midwest. In other words, these species naturally occur within the area and have evolved in this region.

In comparison, exotic, non-native or alien species of plants grow naturally in other geographic regions, such as Europe and Asia, but have been transported to our region. Temperature, rainfall, mountain ranges, deserts and oceans naturally limit the distribution of living things to a certain area. Humans have bypassed the natural barriers and introduced many plants and animals to areas outside of their natural ranges. In many cases, exotic plant species have diminished or displaced native species—native plants that wildlife depend on.

Keep in mind the environmental and ethical significance of choosing which types of plants to buy. When planting flowers, shrubs or trees, many of us feel an inner satisfaction that we are improving the health of our planet. But if these plants aren't native to our region, are we really in tune with nature? Some exotic species can be appropriate on your property, especially in vegetable gardens, perennial flower beds near the house and herb gardens. But to attract wildlife and promote healthy ecosystems, you'll want to grow native plants, not exotics.

Choose From More Than 3,000

Prevailing weather patterns determine the major plant communities found in the Midwest and, therefore, the plant diversity. Weather fronts moving from west to east across the United States lose most of their moisture in the Rocky Mountains, resulting in dry weather patterns for the plains of Kansas. Prairie grasses that grow on these plains require less water than trees.

As these fronts move through the lower Midwest, they regain moisture from the Gulf of Mexico, resulting in enough rainfall to support drought-tolerant trees, such as many species of oaks and hickories. Missouri is in the transition zone between western prairies or grasslands and eastern forests. States to the east and south of Missouri receive more rainfall and will support thirstier trees, such as beech and tulip poplars. Because this area has both prairies and forests, more than 3,000 different species of native plants grow in the central lower Midwest. Native cardinal flowers, beard-tongues, primroses, rattlesnake masters, paintbrushes, shooting stars, turtleheads and catchflies rival the beauty of cultivated species taken from almost anywhere else in the world.

Jim Rathert

CHAPTER COVER PAGE *Coreopsis can be readily established in gardens or flower beds. It prefers full sun and excellent drainage, but it grows well in poor soil.* **ABOVE** *The Midwest is blessed with a great diversity of habitats and plants, such as these stunning cardinal flowers that grow in wet, low-lying areas. If you familiarize yourself with habitat types found in your area, the task of choosing native plants for your property will become easier.*

Balance Natives and Exotics

Seeking a good balance of types of plants on your property is the goal. You probably inherited a variety of native and exotic plants when you obtained your land. In fact, about 800 exotic plants grow wild in Missouri and many hundred more are cultivated in our region, but not all have escaped cultivation nor invaded natural communities. Fortunately, most of these exotics are not aggressive and do not cause major environmental problems. However, when you begin adding plants to your property, choose native plants. They are often easier to grow, help attract wildlife and help restore native habitat.

Natives Have Midwestern Roots

Native plants have evolved in our climate and are adapted to the rainfall, temperatures and soil conditions here. They are equipped to survive the stresses of drought, summer and winter temperatures and our variety of soil conditions without much extra care. Of course, it is still important, even with native species, to put the right plant in the right place—where the plant's moisture, soil and light requirements are met. Native plants can compete with other native species and resist diseases and pests encountered in the Midwest. Although some exotic varieties of flowers and bushes need extra water and fertilizer, most native plants—once established—do not need to be pampered.

Not only are many native plants beautiful, but they form the ecological base for the forest and prairie communities of the region. Native plants and animals have evolved together and are interdependent. Many people know the

Conservationist Aldo Leopold perhaps said it best when he wrote, "The last word in ignorance is the man who says of animal or plant: 'What good is it?' If the land mechanism as a whole is good, then every part is good, whether we understand it or not."

Jim Rathert

relationships between acorns and deer and turkey, flower pollination and insects, berries and our migrating songbirds, and milkweeds and monarch butterflies. When it comes to woodland wildflowers, few people know about the important role that some ants have in the dispersal of seeds for plants such as spring beauties, trilliums, wild ginger and violets. Native plants and animals have achieved a purpose, role or niche in the environment, and their presence and well-being improve the health of the ecosystem and bring balance.

Native Plants Attract Native Wildlife

If you plant them, they will come. Many native wild animals have strategies and mechanisms to collect food from native plants. For many, timing is important. To provision the hive early in the spring, bumblebees, for example, gather pollen from blueberry and farkleberry flowers in special pollen baskets located on their hind legs. These pollinated flowers produce summer blueberries and farkleberries for chipmunks and foxes. When many young birds and mammals are developing in the summer, butterflies and hummingbirds get nectar from blazing stars and milkweeds with their long mouth parts and bills. Early in the fall, flowering dogwood and sassafras leaves begin to turn red and yellow, signaling to migrating cedar waxwings and thrushes that their energy-rich berries are ripe for the picking. Except for maybe wind-pollinated plants, every native flower species in the Midwest has evolved adaptations or strategies to get native animal species to pollinate their flowers or disperse their seeds.

Grow Native! is a landscaping program developed by the Missouri Department of Conservation in cooperation with midwestern nurseries and related businesses. Grow Native! encourages use of native plant materials to enhance biodiversity and increase habitat, reduce maintenance and support quality environmental practices. For more information about Grow Native! and for a list of participating nurseries that sell Midwest native plant materials, send a self-addressed, stamped envelope to Grow Native!, P.O. Box 104671, Jefferson City, MO 65110. Visit the Grow Native! website at www.conservation.state.mo.us/ programs/grownative/

LEFT *As adults, monarch butterflies feed upon the nectar of a variety of plants, although New England aster is especially favored in the fall. While they are in the larval stage—or caterpillars—they are much more choosy and feed only on milkweeds. Adult monarchs are probably the best known butterfly species in North America, largely for their spectacular migration. In the fall, flocks of thousands of the orange and black butterflies fly south to Mexico.*

Jim Rathert

Restore Natural Biodiversity With Natives

As the human population expands, so does the consumption of resources. Biodiversity, the number or variety of different species that exists in an area, is reduced by this consumption.

With new developments and a changing landscape, natural communities become more fragmented. About 98 percent of our vast North American prairies are gone. Plants and animals need connectivity with others of their kind. Your property can be part of that connection.

Planting native wildflowers, shrubs and trees helps restore the natural biodiversity. As a home landscaper, if you begin practicing stronger conservation techniques on your property, asking for and seeking out natives, and landscaping with wildlife in mind, then you, too, can boast that you "think globally, act locally."

Genetic Diversity Counts, Too

When planting natives, try to get plants that have been grown from seed and have originated from your region.

ABOVE *It is a wonderful treat to come across a giant, adult luna moth. As adults, they live for just two weeks or less, and they are most active around midnight. They live in forested areas and feed on walnut, hickory, persimmon and sweet gum trees.* **RIGHT, TOP** *Crab spiders are harmless to people, but readily prey on insect pollinators. Concealed in flowers, they lie in wait to ambush insects that come seeking nectar or pollen.* **RIGHT, BOTTOM** *Some plants earned their common names from the animals that feed upon them. These butterflies are feeding on a sun-loving flower called butterflyweed.*

Dave Tylka

Most seed-grown plants or the actual seeds have a random complement of genes from two different parent plants.

If you obtain plants that came from your local region, you increase your chances of getting plants with genes that are more adapted to your local climate and soils. Native grass seed from your region has a better chance of thriving in your yard than would native grass brought from a different part of the country.

On the other hand, cultivars at nurseries are usually grown from cuttings, making them genetic clones of the parent plants. Cultivars are grown for specific characteristics—such as height, compactness or leaf color—but, in the process, the plant's ability to adapt to changing environmental conditions is more limited.

Native Plants Are Our Heritage

The vast prairies and virgin forests that greeted early settlers to the Midwest have all but disappeared from our landscape. These natural communities are an integral part of our history and natural heritage. Native peoples taught European settlers how to ease toothaches with coneflower roots. Midwest hardwoods played a major role in our country's early transportation needs. Mighty oaks fueled riverboats and supported railroad lines that united east and west. The orientation of sunflowers and compass plants helped to guide covered wagons traveling through tall seas of grass. Spicebush berries flavored pioneer dinners and horsetail stalks were used as early scouring pads after dinner. And where would baseball be without bats carved from ash trees?

Jim Rathert

Jim Rathert

Some Exotics Displace and Disrupt Natural Communities

Native plants contribute to balanced, healthy, natural habitats. Exotic plant species do not.

Although many exotic plants cannot thrive or even survive outside of cultivation here, more than 1,000 non-native species currently are growing wild in the Midwest. Dozens of invasive exotics that come from similar latitudes find the climate very suitable and have caused and are still causing major problems. Bush or Amur honeysuckle, kudzu, autumn olive, multiflora rose, Johnson grass, purple loosestrife, crown vetch, field bindweed and Japanese honeysuckle all are native to Europe and Asia. These highly adaptable and aggressive exotic plants have taken over some of our landscape, displacing native plants, disrupting local ecosystems and causing economic strain.

Evidence from a study in Illinois suggests that the decline of some songbirds, such as wood thrushes and robins, may be linked to exotic shrubs. Exotic honeysuckle and buckthorn shrubs have sturdier branches than many native shrubs. Sturdy branches can help nest predators such as raccoons climb higher to reach nests.

Jim Rathert

Jim Rathert

Some Exotics Attract Wildlife

Wildlife is attracted to many exotic plant species. Some excellent nectar sources for butterflies and hummingbirds are exotics, such as butterfly bush, cypress vine, salvia and simple varieties of zinnias and marigolds. Exotics with fruits or seeds attractive to wildlife are more likely to spread. If these species are already planted on your property or if you decide to use them in your landscape, try to locate them in areas where it will be difficult for them to escape into the wild.

Eliminating the Exotics

Many of the European and Asian exotics that give us grief out-compete our native species because they can germinate under a wide range of conditions, grow quickly, flower early and produce many seeds. In their own native lands, these aggressive plants have been held in check by equally aggressive competitors and tough herbivores—especially insects—that have adapted alongside them. Transported beyond their natural range and away from the species that keep them in check, exotics are primed to invade.

LEFT *Many native plant landscapers find themselves battling exotic species, such as this Oriental bittersweet.* **ABOVE, TOP** *Removing exotic plants from your property, such as this bush honeysuckle, will help your individual natives along and contribute to the over-all health and balance of your habitats.* **ABOVE, BOTTOM** *Not all exotics escape cultivation, but many do. Teasel originally was planted and harvested to make spindles used to raise the nap of woolen cloth. It has become abundant on roadsides and out-competes other more beneficial species.*

Jim Rathert

Past efforts to control exotics have relied heavily upon synthetic herbicides, many of which have harmful side effects on native plants, fish, wildlife and humans. The cost of these chemicals has skyrocketed, not to mention the labor involved in applying them. Millions of dollars of taxpayers' monies are spent annually on the control of exotics.

Regional Agencies and Businesses Promote Native Plants

In the past, government agencies promoted the use of some aggressive exotics, such as bush honeysuckle and multiflora rose, for attracting wildlife and erosion control. However, as knowledge about the risks of introducing exotic species into ecosystems has grown, these policies have changed. Today, many state conservation and natural resources agencies promote the planting of native species on public and private lands. The Missouri Department of Conservation, for example, established a policy in 1997 that not only promotes natives, but prohibits the use of specific exotic plants on department lands.

The nursery industry, too, is evolving from their past dependence on cultivated varieties of exotics to more native plants. Nurseries in the Midwest are increasing their native stock each year, and several specialize in raising and selling only native wildflowers, shrubs and trees. A list of native plant nurseries appears on page 174.

Problem Exotic Wildlife

Besides plants, some animals introduced into our region are also creating environmental havoc. European zebra mussels are clogging public water intake systems and displacing our native mussel species. Exotic crayfish, left over from fishing trip bait buckets, have been dumped into the upper St. Francis River watershed in Missouri and have displaced the smaller native crayfish. The Asian long-horned beetle from China and Korea, with a preference for maples, birches, willows and elms, may eventually cause billions of dollars of damage to urban and suburban shade trees.

Without the barriers and natural forces that help keep populations of exotics in balance in their native lands, gypsy moths, Formosan termites, killer bees, fire ants and nutria (cousins to beavers) all are causing disruptions to natural systems in the U.S. Even the fungus that causes dogwood anthracnose, which has killed 80 percent of the eastern U.S. dogwoods and now threatens Midwest dogwoods, comes from East Asia.

Beneficial Natives

As you've read by now, there are many ecological and ethical reasons to plant natives on your property. Native landscapes are both beautiful and beneficial to a wide array of wildlife throughout the seasons. Begin learning more about natives by visiting a local native plant nursery (many nurseries are listed on page 174) and natural communities near your home for landscaping ideas. It does take an investment of time to learn about the native plants in your region and some trial and error to see for yourself which ones are a match for your tastes and landscape, but it is an investment that will provide you with hours of enjoyment to come.

Expanded global trade threatens to increase the numbers of exotic species invading our country. According to the U.S. Office of Technology Assessment, more than 4,500 exotic species exist in the country and, "by the mid-21st century, biological invasions will become one of the most prominent ecological issues on earth."

LEFT *In some places, such as this stretch of Highway 54 in Cole County, Missouri, state highway departments have planted wildflowers along roadsides in place of fescue or other non-native turf. Wildflowers reduce the need and costs for mowing, benefit tourism and improve biodiversity. Communicate with your county and state highway officials and encourage them to use native wildflowers and grasses along public roadways.*

Cliff White

plan and design before you dig

Chapter Three

*M*any enthusiastic wildlife gardeners have been guilty of
jumping into a backyard landscaping project with broad ideas in
mind, but few real plans. They may have purchased a wildlife plant
recommended by a friend or one seen in a newspaper article and
planted them without much thought. Later, many of these plants
had to be moved because they got too big, didn't grow well in the
conditions, or it turned out to be an aggressive plant that started to
take over the yard. Plants can be moved if they are found to be in
the wrong place, but relocated shrubs and trees take about a year
to recover from the stress of being and replanted.

For those who are new to wildlife landscaping, this chapter
introduces you to some basic planning concepts. At the beginning,
coming up with a comprehensive plan may seem a bit overwhelming,
but breaking it down into these six steps simplifies the process.

Assess sun, soil and moisture conditions.
Inventory existing plants and nearby plant communities.
Anticipate your use of the land.
Anticipate the level of maintenance.
Consider various designs and arrangements.
Prioritize and schedule plantings.

While you don't want to go overboard with planning, a sketch or
two and some quick site analysis will pay off later, in both time
and money.

step 1: *Assess Sun, Soil and Moisture Conditions*

Among seasoned landscapers and gardeners, one of the oldest sayings is, "Always put the right plant in the right place." What makes one location right and another wrong? The three most important physical factors that influence whether a plant thrives, survives or dies are the amount of light, the soil conditions and the amount of moisture.

SUN

Start by walking around your yard with paper and pencil in hand. On a base map, sketch the location of your home, any buildings or structures and any groupings of plants, especially trees. Although it will vary with each season, mark areas that receive at least six hours of direct sun, areas of full shade and areas inbetween that receive partial sun or shade. Plants need different amounts of sun to flower and fruit properly, so this sketch will be an important reference when you select species to plant.

SOIL

The soil pH and composition determine what types of plants will prosper in your yard. Most garden plants prefer a neutral to slightly acidic pH and a nutrient-rich loam soil. But native plants are adapted to a wide range of soil pH and nutrient levels. Sandy soils tend to drain quickly while clay soils tend to hold moisture and

CHAPTER COVER PAGE *Whether you have a single native flower bed or several acres to work with, there's nothing like seeing the rewards of your labor appear in brilliant reds, purples and yellows of various wildflowers.*

Analyzing your landscaping site and drawing a couple of sketches will pay off, both in time and money.

nutrients. If your home is fairly new and the builder did not save the topsoil by moving it to the side and replacing it after construction, you may have to bring topsoil in from another source. Heavy clay soils that originate deep under the topsoil and stick together in your hands offer the biggest challenge. Sand, gypsum, well-decomposed compost or manure (fresh compost and manure typically contain too many weed seeds) and peat moss may need to be added to your soil to support healthy plant growth. If you have doubts about the quality of the soil, call your county University Outreach and Extension Service for instructions on how to collect soil samples and get them analyzed. There is usually a small fee. The results list soil conditions and suggestions for remedying any soil deficiencies.

MOISTURE

You may want to jot down moisture conditions on your base map, too. Note the places that tend to hold water after a heavy rain or slopes that drain quickly. Red and white oaks that typically grow on slopes and ridge tops are adapted to well-drained soils, but pin and willow oaks, which generally are found on bottomlands, prefer to keep their feet wet in soils that retain moisture. When you select plants, moisture requirements help determine the right plant for the right place. Any areas with soil erosion should also be marked on your map because some plant species have large root systems that can help stabilize problem areas.

RIGHT *Field guides are the ticket to identifying plants that may be unfamiliar to you, such as this lanceleaf coreopsis. You likely will be amazed at the number of different plants species you'll find on your property, and the resulting inventory will help you plan and design new native landscapes.*

step 2: *Inventory Existing Plants and Nearby Plant Communities*

Think back to the concepts of connectivity and wildlife corridors introduced in Chapter One on page 16. Where is your yard located? Look to see if your home is linked to local forests or open prairie or meadow communities. If you live in the suburbs, is your neighborhood dominated by large clumps of older trees or open grasslands? Or perhaps you live close to a wooded creek, nature park or forested, subdivision grounds. Is the area surrounding your home made up of mowed and unmowed yards, ballfields, golf courses or cemetery grounds (open, sunny areas)? Maybe you live amid a mix or mosaic of shade and sun habitats; there are patches of both large trees and open, grassy areas dotted with flowerbeds. Making your property an extension of any nearby natural community increases your chances of attracting the local wildlife to your yard.

After you have a feel for nature in your neighborhood, inventory the common plants on your property. Record the larger, more dominant vegetation on the base map, noting shrub and tree species if you can identify them. There are several good field guides for identifying native trees, shrubs and wildflowers that can be obtained free from public agencies, checked out of the library or purchased locally. If you need help with shrub or

Jim Rathert

Jim Rathert

tree identification, collect a 10-inch branch with leaves, fold it into a sealed plastic bag to prevent the leaves from drying out and take it to a nearby nursery, forestry office or nature center.

Completing the inventory all at once isn't essential, but it does help you learn more about native plants and discover which ones are valuable to wildlife for food and cover. Chapters Four and Five go into detail about preferred native wildlife plants. Before you decide to cut down trees or shrubs that represent many years of growth, consult other wildlife gardeners or reference books regarding their wildlife value. Although some tree species do not benefit wildlife directly, their shade and cooling effect may furnish habitat for native woodland wildflowers, reduce your home's energy needs and be a real asset to your property.

step 3: Anticipate Your Use of the Land

CURRENT USE

Think about how you and others in your household use your property. On your base map or on a clear plastic overlay, mark the areas where you feed birds, entertain, garden, park vehicles, play, read or even sneak in a nap. Be sure to include any activities that can be seen, heard or smelled. Record any views that you want to protect or screen and any bothersome noises from traffic or neighbors. Wind direction is important, too, especially if you store garbage cans outside, grill, maintain a compost pile or have pets. If dogs and cats regularly have the run of the yard, keep in mind they will inhibit wildlife interactions on your property.

FUTURE USE

Besides the way you currently use your property, think about activities you may want to do in the future. Do you plan to build an addition? Which yard activities are the most important? Are they compatible within your space? You probably want to locate quiet areas where you feed birds or nap away from noisier areas where you entertain or play with kids or pets. In small yards, consider using fences or bushes to separate activity areas.

INSIDE LOOKING OUT

After walking around and analyzing your yard from the outside, go inside your home. Although the mild weather and colors of spring and autumn draw you outdoors, most of your time at home is probably spent inside. Therefore, go around to rooms where you spend daytime hours, such as the study, breakfast nook or dinner table. Make sure the views from these rooms are clear and unobstructed. Catching periodic glimpses of cardinals, black swallowtails or humming-birds can enliven washing dishes or working at the computer.

Be sure to locate birdfeeders, water gardens and wildflower beds where you can enjoy the action from a favorite window. Your home conceals you from the wildlife and can serve as a photography or observation blind as long as you stay back a couple of feet from the window. You can watch or photograph many types of animal behaviors from the comfort of your home.

Jim Rathert

LEFT *Read a book? Play a game of catch? Build a place to barbecue? There are endless ways to enjoy the outdoors on your property, and these activities will influence your landscaping designs.* **ABOVE** *The views from inside are just as important as the views from the outside, especially as the seasons change and bring new color, such as the lush, pinkish-red of this Eastern redbud in full bloom.*

Tell your neighbors about your landscaping plans. You may avert conflict and, even better, you may help kindle in them an interest in native landscaping, too.

WINNING OVER THE NEIGHBORHOOD

Think, too, about how your plantings will be viewed by neighbors. Will they be accepting of your plan? Can you help others nearby develop similar landscape habitats to expand your efforts and corridors? Once your shade and sun perennials are established, there are always a few seedlings or seed to share. Being a native plant ambassador can become a big part of the fun. A few plants can make a convert of a friend and be the seed for a new hobby. Soon, they'll be joining you in the planning, shopping and planting of more species.

step 4: Anticipate the Level of Maintenance

STARTING FROM SCRATCH

If you live in a new subdivision or plan to convert large areas of lawn into native landscaping, get ready for many hours of maintenance caring for your new plants and keeping down the competition from unwanted plants. Large-scale changes to your landscape can be rewarding but require much work if you do it yourself, or great expense if you hire others. Instead, you may want to ease gradually into establishing native sun and shade landscapes.

Whenever you expose and disturb the soil, you bring some weed seeds to the surface where they will germinate and compete with the plants you want there. This is especially challenging if your planting site was once an old field that probably has many dormant weed seeds. The amount of time you commit to weeding depends on how tolerant you are to unwanted plants, how much you disturb the soil and how much mulch you spread around your plants to keep the weeds down. Newly planted wildflowers, shrubs and trees generally need extra watering for about a month until they become accustomed to their new location.

Paul Childress

CHANGING OLD LANDSCAPES

The maintenance level drops if you already have some shade and sun landscapes and you just want to revitalize these areas with native plantings. Shaded, forested landscapes have fewer invasions from many weeds. Mulch will further reduce weed growth and will help retain moisture for new plantings.

Some large trees may create seasonal chores. Trees such as mulberries produce squishy fruits that can stain walking surfaces or cars. Other trees produce nuts and acorns that land on nearby sidewalks, patios and decks or in gutters. Sweeping hard-surfaced walkways will reduce your chances of falling, and cleaning out gutters or installing gutter guards or catch-free guttering will avoid clogs and overflows.

Sun landscapes usually require more weeding than shade landscapes, thanks to the sun's energy and the openness to airborne weed seeds, although mulching helps. Once a prairie or perennial meadow is established—usually in about three to five years—maintenance drops, too. But again, this depends on your tolerance for unwanted plants.

MULCHING

Not only does mulch reduce weed growth, it also helps hold moisture, maintains the temperature around the roots and prevents soil compaction. With these conditions, aeration and water absorption are improved. Rather than using gravel as cover, lean toward organic mulches, such as wood chips, shredded bark and compost to help recycle yard wastes back into the environment. Avoid using freshly shredded wood products or compost that hasn't aged. As bacteria and fungi begin decomposing the wood, they use up

Native trees, shrubs, grasses and wildflowers require little watering and no applications of insecticides or fertilizers. Once established, most people find native landscaping is less expensive and time-consuming to maintain than expansive mowed lawns and ornamentals.

LEFT *Not all your native landscaping projects have to be large in scale or especially time-consuming. There are plenty of ways to take advantage of small spaces and limited time and still succeed in attracting wildlife; many are covered in Chapter Six, "Bird and Butterfly Landscapes," and the "Quick Tips" in Chapter Nine.*

Pat Whalen

many of the nutrients in the soil needed by your plants. Fresh wood chips can be used on paths or trails, or you may stockpile fresh chips downwind from your house and allow them to decompose thoroughly before use. As insurance, many people sprinkle basic fertilizer on the ground around plants before spreading organic mulches.

Plants that gain the most from mulch are those with shallow root systems such as flowering dogwoods, plants with leaves that droop or turn color during summer droughts such as river birches or tulip trees, and evergreens such as the Eastern red cedar that turn brown during dry winters. An inch or two of well-decomposed compost mulch works best around more delicate wildflowers and ferns, but a four- to six-inch layer of coarser bark and wood mulch is best around shrubs and trees. Periodically check mulch for compaction, and loosen the material if it develops into a firm layer. Here is a tip: Replenish mulch around plants or on trails in winter when it is much more enjoyable to work in cool, crisp weather than during our steamy summers.

step 5: *Consider Various Designs, Arrangements*

SKETCH ON PAPER

By now, you probably have a good idea of where you would like to create more shade by adding trees, as well as where you would like to brighten sunny areas by planting wildflowers, grasses, shrubs and vines. As you begin to consider the exact locations for trees, remember that a small one- to two-inch diameter tree

ABOVE *There are several species of coneflowers native to the Midwest, and they are favorites among city as well as rural landscapers. They grow easily and if you "dead-head" them—that is, snip off the dead flowers once they have bloomed and wilted—new flowers will appear and bloom over again for many weeks during the summer and fall.* **RIGHT** *Landscaping with native plants doesn't mean your beds or designs have to look too "wild" or messy. Take advantage of grasses and flowers that are complimentary in appearance and blooming times.*

that you plant today may grow very large and affect the growth and flowering ability of other vegetation for decades to come. Many species, such as oaks and maples, spread out to widths of about 50 feet, so keep width as well as height in mind when laying out a shaded landscape plan.

To get a better idea on paper of how trees will grow and shade your yard, cut out circles of colored paper to represent the size of various tree species and lay them on your base map. Do these circles cover up other plants or impact yard activities? Move the circles around on your base map to see how different groupings appeal to you aesthetically. To help visualize the new landscape, some people use photographs of their property and sketch in trees and shrubs with water-soluble pens or even purchase computer software programs that have graphics capabilities. Remember to strive for plant diversity and to keep landscape views in mind. Again, locate your water features and bird feeding stations near your house if you want to get a clear view of the wildlife activity from your windows.

After plotting tree locations, sketch the locations for shrubs, vines and prairie or meadow-type wildflowers and grasses. Sun-loving plants need at least six hours of sun per day for good bloom and fruit production for wildlife. Sun landscapes may vary in size from large expanses of prairie wildflowers and grasses to small beds of verbena or coneflowers.

Dave Tylka

Jim Rathert

TRICKS TO HELP YOU VISUALIZE

To help you visualize what your yard will become, spread out ropes, garden hoses or tarps in different places to represent wildflower and grass areas. Lawn chairs, buckets or clay pots can stand for various sizes of trees and shrubs. To estimate areas, some gardeners use chalk or water-soluble spray paint, but these cannot be moved as easily as ropes and chairs.

Continue to move your vegetation models around until everything looks pleasing from all angles and also from the inside of your home. With larger yards or small acreages, your design options increase dramatically (see Chapter Eight). You can plant trees in islands or clumps, in hedgerows or windbreaks and in large groupings that closely resemble a natural forest community.

STRIVE FOR DIVERSITY

Generally, to attract the greatest diversity of native wildlife, plant a diversity of native plants. Getting wild animals to notice your yard, though, is important. Plant several individuals of one particular plant close to each other to help draw wildlife to your yard. If your yard is flat, give it some relief by digging out and creating low, moist areas. Pile the soil into a hill-like mound or a meandering, elevated berm that can double as a visual and sound screen along a noisy property line.

When selecting flowering plant species, choose a diversity of plants that flower at different times of the year so nectar feeders, such as butterflies, have food from spring to fall. Phlox and aromatic sumacs bloom early. Coneflowers and buttonbushes come next. New England asters and blue lobelias flower late (see Chapters Four and Five).

ABOVE *Be sure to include a birdbath or watering hole in your landscaping plans. Wildlife is especially attracted to sources of continuously available water.* **RIGHT** *The cardinal flower is a member of the bellflower family and hard to beat for its brilliance and contrast against a green backdrop of shrubs and trees. It perfers moist to wet soils.*

Jim Rathert

PATHS OR TRAILS

To help you enjoy your native plants and the wildlife they bring, consider adding paths or trails to your plan. This is especially important if you have large areas of shade and sun landscapes and you want to access them for weeding and clipping. Avoid running your paths at right angles or in straight lines. Instead, meanders in your path lead to new discoveries around the next sweeping bend.

Organic materials such as wood chips are environmentally friendly to use for trail surfaces, and most municipalities and tree care companies have chips available for free. In most areas, yard wastes are prohibited from being dumped in landfills so public supplies of mulch are often plentiful. To make a trail surface, apply a two- to four-inch layer of coarse, hardwood chips (from oaks and hickories) first, as a stable base. Over the top, you can dress up the chips with more finely cut bark mulch or compost.

DESIGN LIKE NATURE

When shaping flowerbed edges or places where groups of plants meet, avoid straight lines and perpendicular corners. Nature tends not to plant in straight lines nor space out plants perfectly, especially in groups of two and four. For small clusters, groups of three and five look less contrived. Stairstep your plantings by arranging them in tiers—locating the taller species in the background and the shorter ones in the foreground.

step 6: *Prioritize and Schedule Plantings*

EXERCISE PATIENCE

Landscaping companies can help you develop and implement a landscape plan quickly. The downside of hiring out for this work is, of course, the cost. For most of us, enhancing our landscape for wildlife takes time. We begin by putting up a birdfeeder or two, planting a few species of trees or selecting and landscaping one area of the yard, before moving on to the next. If certain plant species do not grow well in one location after a reasonable amount of time, move them to another site and replace them with something more adapted to the soil, light

and moisture conditions. Achieving the right balance of species in your shade and sun landscapes takes time. Exercise patience.

SCHEDULE PLANTINGS

The best times to plant trees and shrubs are in the spring and fall. Before planting trees that are large, long-lived and hard to transplant, make sure that you are happy with the characteristics of the tree species and the locations. Remember the fruits, too, and how they will fall in your yard. Many trees and shrubs take several years of growth before they begin to flower and fruit well enough to attract wildlife. If there is a good chance that you'll move in the next few years, you may want to plant more perennial wildflowers and grasses for quicker results. If you are not certain about how long you'll own your home, plant some in each category.

When planting seeds for native wildflower perennials that are adapted to sun, begin in the early winter so seeds can go through the freeze and thaw cycles necessary for many of these species to germinate. Native, warm-season grass seeds may be planted from the early winter throughout spring. When grown from seed, most native wildflowers put their energy into root development the first year or two and generally will not flower until the third year, with the exception of Black-eyed Susans.

If you must have flowering during the first year, buy two-year-old perennial wildflowers as bare-rooted plants or in pots or plugs and plant them in early April. The soil around the new plants should be kept moist for the first six to eight weeks when the young plants are susceptible to drought. Afterward, they are fairly self-sustaining. For more information on planting wildflowers, detailed information is provided in Chapter Five on sun landscapes.

Jim Rathert

Jim Rathert

KEEP NOTES

As your plantings and the seasons progress, keep notes on what you've accomplished and how the plantings grew—especially what worked and what didn't do well. You may also want to use your notes as a journal to record wildlife sightings through the seasons. Before putting a new section of your plan into action each spring, review your notes and modify the plans as needed.

DEVELOP REALISTIC EXPECTATIONS

The level of investment, enjoyment and success of your native landscaping is a personal matter. But be realistic in your expectations. At first, your expectations may be satisfied by a few bird and butterfly species visiting your yard and maybe a mockingbird, robin or bluejay nest. You may start out by wanting to get a dozen different bird species to visit your yard. Then, as you gain more knowledge and experience, you may specifically plant butterfly milkweed for monarchs or pawpaw trees for zebra swallowtail butterflies. As mentioned before, connections and proximity to other natural communities will affect the wildlife you attract, so build your expectations with all of this in mind.

LEFT *When choosing plants that will be prominently placed, be sure to check when they flower and how long they stay in bloom. Take advantage of their natural timing to ensure that something is in bloom all season.*
ABOVE *Don't forget insects are wildlife, too. Tune in to the insect species that visit your yard, such as this skipper resting on a rough blazing star. Many insects are beautiful as well as essential food sources for countless birds, mammals and amphibians.*

shade landscapes

Chapter Four

*F*orests, woods and woodlands are types of shade landscapes. Here, shade landscapes are defined as natural or natural-like groupings of native plants dominated by large- to medium-sized trees. Shade landscapes, such as forests and woods, are also characterized by a wide range of different plant species, or biodiversity. These include a variety of woodland wildflowers, ferns, shrubs and trees. Increased plant diversity increases wildlife diversity. To maximize the benefits to wildlife, strive to plant or nurture a wide diversity of plants.

Wood lots, groves and tree farms are not considered shade landscapes because they lack biodiversity. Although wood lots and tree farms provide some wildlife habitat, the reduced biodiversity means fewer wildlife species use the area. These areas tend to be evenly spaced groupings of one or two species of trees, planted and managed primarily for the harvest of a product. To maximize harvest in wood lots, other plant species are commonly removed to reduce competition.

Layers of Vegetation

In shade landscapes, you may find up to four layers of vegetation: the canopy (overstory branches and leaves of the taller trees), the understory (branches and leaves of the shorter trees), the shrubs or bushes and the ground vegetation (including woodland wildflowers and ferns). All plants need sunlight to grow and be healthy. To avoid being shaded by the taller trees in the forest, some native woodland plant species become active early in the spring before the trees leaf out. Their strategy is to produce flowers early in the spring while sunlight still reaches the forest floor. Native wildflowers, several understory trees, such as serviceberry and flowering dogwood, and a few shrubs, such as spicebush, all bloom in March and April.

Paula Kapfer

Other woodland plants require less amounts of sunlight. Unlike the thick canopies of maple forests to the east, Midwest oak and hickory forests typically have small gaps in their canopies, allowing some sunlight to trickle through their leaves. This is referred to as filtered sunlight. Some plants can survive in the low light. Understory trees, such as red buckeye and pawpaw, shrubs such as aromatic sumac, and native blueberries and wildflowers such as touch-me-nots, can live in filtered sunlight. However, many of these bushes and understory trees have increased flower and fruit production if they are located at the edge of the woods or underneath an opening in the canopy.

CHAPTER COVER PAGE *Shady landscapes around your home help keep it cool in summer, as well as help it appear inviting. It is natural to think horizontally when you plan landscapes, but consider the vertical landscape, too. Native plants and trees grow to varying heights and alter views and vistas. For wildlife, not all the action is on the ground, either. Many species use high places in trees for feeding and nesting.*

Conservation areas, state parks and wildlife refuges in your region are good places to find inspiration and learn about native landscapes.

In a forest with large, mature trees, the bush and understory layers may be sparse or absent because of the lack of sunlight. If you already have large mature trees in your yard, you may want to focus on the ground layer and consider understory trees and bushes only around the edges of the large trees.

Visit Midwest Forests for Ideas and Inspiration

Wildlife activity varies during each season. Visit a local forest or woodland at different times of the year to observe first-hand what occurs there. Try to get an overview of what nature offers its inhabitants through the seasons, and especially watch to see how wildlife use flowers and fruits. Bring home ideas from the forest and try to imitate the attractive components and the diversity of the forest landscape on your property. Check the tables in this book for other wildlife species that are attracted to the plants you observed in the forest. Find out how tall and wide these plants will become to see if they are suitable for your property. As you begin to put together a wish list of plants for your yard, check with nearby native nurseries—many are listed on page 174—to learn the costs and availability of various species.

If you live along a creek or if water stands in your yard after a good rain, visit a bottomland forest located along a creek or river floodplain in your neighborhood. Bottomland forest trees, such as black gum, birches and pawpaws, are adapted to

RIGHT *Individually, spring beauties and yellow violets are diminutive, but planted together beneath a tree, they blanket the ground in a wash of color. They are examples of wildflowers you may plant when you "start big, work down." Visit a forest or woods near your home to find inspiration and ideas for your shade landscapes.*

moist bottomland soil conditions. If creeks are not near your yard or if you live on a ridge or hill, visit an upland forest. Many species of oaks and dogwoods grow best in dry, well-drained, upland soils. Look for wildlife activity in the four different layers of vegetation.

Identify native plants that furnish the most wildlife food and cover or have unusual features that may add character to your yard, such as bloodroot leaves or Jack-in-the-pulpit flowers. To help identify plants, take along a field guide or camera and visit with staff at a nature center or nursery about those plants that are tough to identify.

Start Big, Work Down

Think tall and begin your shade or woodland landscape plan by first considering the trees that grow 30 feet or taller, and then work your way down to the smaller trees, shrubs and woodland wildflowers. Trees are the foundation of your shade landscape and take many years to grow tall. If you are not sure how long you are going to stay at one location, you may want to glance through the tree sections and instead, focus on shorter, faster growing plants. If you already have a few large trees in your yard, skip ahead to the sections on understory trees, shrubs and woodland wildflowers. Refer to the tables and plant descriptions for wildlife use, site adaptations and dimensions, and landscape characteristics of shade plants.

In a forest environment, tall trees compete with each other for sunlight to produce fruits, berries, seeds and nuts. To be successful, many trees grow taller and wider to gather more sun than their tree neighbors. Therefore, space out the large trees in your yard for better flower and fruit production. Some overlapping branches of mature trees is all right, but avoid crowding

Jim Rathert

Jim Rathert

trees too close. If you need to visually screen off an area, then you may want to plant evergreen trees close together to block the view.

Look High for Action

Similar to the rainforest trees of the tropics, most wildlife activity in mature Midwestern forests during the growing season takes place high in the canopy where the flowers and fruits are produced. Although some trees, such as evergreens and oaks, are wind pollinated, many tree species are insect pollinated. If you have black cherry, tulip poplar, persimmon or maple trees growing next to your house, look high in the branches to observe the diversity of insects—and insect predators—visiting the tree flowers in spring. Binoculars help, but to avoid a stiff neck from frequent birdwatching high in the canopy, lie back on an old blanket or chaise lounge. For a little different view, watch insects and birds from a second-story window or a rooftop vantage point. Tree flowers attract bees, butterflies, beetles and insect-eating birds, such as vireos and warblers, but their visits go unnoticed by most people.

Other wildlife visits trees when the flowers turn into seeds, berries and nuts. Sparrows, thrushes, mocking-birds, squirrels and opossums are attracted to various types of fruits. It is always a treat to watch a flock of cedar waxwings swoop in for the blue berries (actually fleshy cones) of the female Eastern red cedar tree. Other species, such as deer mice, chipmunks, deer and turkey, gather fruits and nuts when they fall to the ground. In the fall, gray and fox squirrels, as well as bluejays, bury extra

acorns in soil for the winter months. Forgotten acorns become new oak trees. Higher on the food chain, foxes, hawks and owls prey on mice, chipmunks or squirrels.

Dead Trees Are Wildlife Habitat, Too

Trees furnish wildlife habitat not only when they are living but also when they die. Standing dead trees are called snags, and fallen dead trees and stumps are referred to as deadwood. Carefully cut down dangerous snags that lean over a path, patio, toward your home or parking areas. Also cut down and burn any snags or deadwood that are infested with transmittable diseases such as Dutch elm disease. Otherwise, allow dead trees to stand upright or fall and decay naturally.

Downy, red-bellied and pileated woodpeckers chisel out holes in snags for homes. Fortunately for other wildlife, woodpeckers use these nest holes only once and construct new holes for their next families. Abandoned woodpecker holes are used by wrens, chickadees, bats, screech owls, flying squirrels and lizards. You can create more wildlife apartments or nest holes in snags with a portable drill. Some people drill small holes in snags or wooden blocks for beneficial solitary bees (see Chapter Nine for tips about attracting insects).

If you want to construct wooden nest boxes, plans for bird, squirrel and bat houses are available from a local conservation office or nature center. Hole size affects the wildlife occupants of both nest boxes and snags. Carefully cut entrance

LEFT *Shagbark hickory trees are known for their intriguing, pealing bark. The textured trunk is full of places where insects and mammals seek shelter and food. Bats, especially, are known to roost under a shagbark "roof." Neighborhood bats are harmless and highly beneficial because they eat mosquitoes and other insects pesky to humans.* **ABOVE** *Flying squirrels are just one of many species that make use of dead tree trunks. These nocturnal mammals are not true flyers; they launch themselves and glide with the help extra folds of skin between their hind and front legs.*

Jim Rathert

holes if you want to favor native birds, such as bluebirds, wrens and chickadees, and discourage non-native, aggressive starlings.

Deadwood and Brushpiles

Chickadees, nuthatches and woodpeckers feed on the insects attracted to decaying wood. Do not clean up the forest floor by removing deadwood. This is nature's way of recycling the organic matter for woodland wildflowers or for the next generation of trees. To create more wildlife cover, many people build brush piles with deadwood. To make compartments within your brush pile, lay large branches on the ground parallel to each other, spaced three to six inches apart. Add additional layers by stacking other branches crosswise. Finally, throw several small branches on the top. These serve as escape cover for small birds, and the compartments can become homes for wrens, sparrows, rabbits, chipmunks, salamanders and lizards.

Deciduous and Evergreen Trees

For diversity, consider planting both deciduous and evergreen trees. Deciduous trees are broad-leaved trees that shed their leaves all at once in the autumn, such as oaks and maples. Evergreen trees, such as pines and cedars, replace their needle-like leaves

Jim Rathert

"Trees properly placed around buildings can reduce air-conditioning needs by 30 percent and can save 20 to 50 percent in energy used for heating," reads a study by the *U.S.D.A. Forest Service. In addition, the Department of Agriculture found that healthy, mature trees can add an average of 10 percent to a property's value.*

Jim Rathert

gradually during the entire year. Because large deciduous trees tend to out-compete the evergreen trees for sun, plant evergreens in groups away from deciduous trees. Birds especially use evergreens for cover at night and during cold weather.

Trees Reduce Energy Costs

To reduce home cooling costs in the summer, locate larger deciduous trees on the south and southwest sides of your house to block the warm sunlight. In the winter when the deciduous tree leaves are off, the warmth of the sunlight reaches the house. To help save on heating costs in the winter, locate evergreens on the north and northwest sides of your house to help block the chilling winds. Besides furnishing wildlife cover, evergreen trees also serve as screens to provide year-round privacy and to reduce traffic or neighborhood noises.

LEFT, TOP *Downy woodpeckers and hairy woodpeckers, like this one feeding on a limb, are common visitors around both rural and suburban landscapes. They search tree trunks for insects and also come readily to suet feeders.* **LEFT, BOTTOM** *Many salamanders, including this spotted salamander, inhabit damp woods, woodland ponds and brush piles. They emerge at night and eat worms, insects, spiders and snails.* **ABOVE** *Tree-lined streets make neighborhoods attractive and set them apart, no matter what size the town or city.*

Large Native Trees

This is a list of trees, 30 feet or more in height, that provide beneficial food and cover for wildlife. Many large trees have long taproots, which make transplanting them a challenge. Keep in mind that soil described as dry generally is found on ridge tops, south- and west-facing slopes and drains quickly. Moist soil drains slowly and includes most urban soils and north- and east-facing slopes. Wet soils are low-lying and often water-saturated.

						HICKORIES		MAPLES		OAKS
NAME	Basswood *Tilia americana*	Black Cherry *Prunus serotina*	Blackgum *Nyssa sylvatica*	Black Willow *Salix nigra*	Hackberry *Celtis occidentalis*	Pecan *Carya illinoensis*	Shagbark Hickory *Carya ovata*	Red Maple *Acer rubrum*	Sugar Maple *Acer saccharum*	Northern Red Oak *Quercus rubra*
SIZE	60 ft. tall 30 ft. wide	65 ft. tall 40 ft. wide	40 ft. tall 25 ft. wide	35 ft. tall 30 ft. wide	60 ft. tall 40 ft. wide	75 ft. tall 50 ft. wide	70 ft. tall 45 ft. wide	55 ft. tall 45 ft. wide	65 ft. tall 40 ft. wide	70 ft. tall 50 ft. wide
WHEN DOES IT FLOWER?	May-July	April-May	April-May	April-May	April-May	April-May	April-May	March-April	April-May	April-May
FLOWER COLOR	yellowish-cream	white	small, green	yellowish-white	small, green	small, green	small, green	red	yellow	small, green
UNIQUE OR ATTRACTIVE FEATURES		fall color	fall color		bark		bark, fall color	bark, fall color	fall color	fall color
WHAT WILDLIFE COVER & FOOD DOES IT PROVIDE?	general cover; insect food, seeds	general cover; butterfly/moth nectar, butterfly/moth larval food, insect food, summer fruit, seeds	general cover; insect food, fall fruit for migrating birds, seeds	general cover, clumps or thickets; insect food, butterfly/moth larval food, seeds	general cover; butterfly/moth larval food, fall fruit for migrating birds, seeds	general cover; butterfly/moth larval food, nuts	general cover; butterfly/moth larval food, nuts	general cover; butterfly/moth larval food, insect food, seeds	general cover; butterfly/moth larval food, insect food, seeds	general cover; butterfly/moth larval food, insect food, acorns
GROWS IN WHAT KIND OF SOIL?	moist	dry, moist	dry, moist, wet	moist	dry, moist	moist, tolerates clay	dry	dry, moist, wet	dry, moist	dry, moist
COMMENTS	Excellent bee tree; honey from flowers highly valued; larval food for several moths; seeds eaten by small mammals such as chipmunks	Songbirds and chipmunks relish berries and disperse seeds; attractive white flower clusters furnish pollen and nectar to insects; larval food for moths (cecropia and sphinx) and butterflies (tiger swallowtail, red-spotted purple)	Songbirds eat berries and disperse seeds; bees pollinate male and female flowers (on separate trees); scarlet fall color; larval source for Hebrew moth; challenging to transplant	Leaves emerge early and provide larval food for butterflies (mourning cloak, viceroy, red-spotted purple) and moths (cecropia, scalloped owlet, sphinxes, underwings); bees pollinate male and female flowers (on separate trees); easy to transplant or start new trees with stem cuttings; stabilizes streambanks; avoid planting near underground pipes or foundations	Songbirds relish berries and disperse seeds; larval food for butterflies (question mark, mourning cloak, tawny emperor, snout, hackberry) and wild cherry sphinx moth; unique elevated warts on bark	Tasty, thin-shelled nut easily cracked and eaten by mammals; larval food for banded hairstreak butterfly and several moths (luna, regal); tolerates short-term flooding; wind pollinated; challenging to transplant	Squirrels and chipmunks eat nuts; loose, shaggy bark used by bats for daytime roosts; larval food for butterflies (hickory, banded hairstreaks) and moths (luna, regal); yellow fall color; wind-pollinated; challenging to transplant	Adapted to wide range of soils (except alkaline); flies and small bees pollinate male and female flowers; larval food for imperial moth; brilliant red and orange fall colors; smooth, gray bark sensitive to fire	Songbirds eat winged fruit containing seeds; variety of insects pollinate; larval food for moths (cecropia, imperial); brilliant red and orange fall colors; sap for maple sugar and syrup	A faster-growing oak; well-adapted to cold weather; large acorns 3/4" to 1" long; larval food for butterflies (hairstreaks, skippers) and moths; harmless walkingsticks relish leaves; wind-pollinated

Pin Oak *Quercus palustris*	White Oak *Quercus alba*	Willow Oak *Quercus phellos*	Ohio Buckeye *Aesculus glabra*	Persimmon *Diospyros virginiana*	Red Mulberry *Morus rubra*	River Birch *Betula nigra*	Sassafras *Sassafras albidum*	Shortleaf Pine *Pinus echinata*	Tuliptree *Liriodendron tulipifera*	White Ash *Fraxinus americana*
65 ft. tall 35 ft. wide	65 ft. tall 50 ft. wide	50 ft. tall 40 ft. wide	35 ft. tall 25 ft. wide	50 ft. tall 25 ft. wide	40 ft. tall 35 ft. wide	50 ft. tall 35 ft. wide	45 ft. tall 30 ft. wide	90 ft. tall 60 ft. wide	80+ ft. tall 40 ft. wide	65 ft. tall 40 ft. wide
April-May	April-May	April-May	April-May	May-June	April-May	April-May	April-May		April-May	April-May
small, green	small, green	small, green	greenish-yellow	yellowish-white	small, green	small, green	small, yellow		yellow and orange	small, purple
fall color	fall color		leaves		leaves	bark	leaves, fall color	leaves	leaves	fall color
general cover; butterfly/moth larval food, insect food, acorns	general cover; butterfly/moth larval food, insect food, acorns	general cover; butterfly/moth larval food, insect food, acorns	hummingbird nectar, seeds	general cover, clumps or thickets; butterfly/moth larval food, insect food, winter fruit, seeds	general cover; insect food, summer fruit	general cover; insect food, butterfly/moth larval food, seeds	clumps or thickets; butterfly/moth larval food, insect food, fall fruit for migrating birds	general cover, evergreen; butterfly/moth larval food, seeds	general cover; insect food, hummingbird nectar, seeds	general cover; butterfly/moth larval food, seeds
moist, wet, tolerates clay	dry, moist, tolerates clay	moist, wet, tolerates clay	moist	dry, moist	dry, moist	moist, wet, tolerates clay	dry, moist	dry, grows well in acidic, nutrient-poor soil	moist	dry, moist, wet
A faster-growing oak; most widely used oak for landscaping; small acorns 1/2" long; larval food for butterflies (hairstreaks, skippers) and moths; wind-pollinated	Slow-growing, long-lived tree; acorns 1/2" to 3/4" long; larval food for butterflies (hairstreaks, skippers) and moths; wind-pollinated; challenging to transplant	Fast-growing, narrow-leaved oak; small acorn less than 1/2" long eaten by small mammals and birds; larval food for butterflies (hairstreaks, skippers) and moths; wind-pollinated; not winter hardy north of Missouri River	Showy flowers furnish nectar for hummingbirds; frost-resistant leaves emerge early in spring with leaflets attached in circular (palmate) pattern; tree named for large, hard nuts called buckeyes	Mammals, especially opossums, and fruit-eating birds eat fleshy, orange fruits and disperse seeds; bees pollinate male and female flowers; larval food for moths (luna, regal); ripe fruit can be used in jellies and breads	Birds and mammals relish fleshy berries (resemble skinny blackberries) that ripen different times over several-week period; insects pollinate male and female flowers (on separate trees); fruits can be messy around walkways, driveways, patios; ripe fruits suitable for jellies, wines, etc.	Young trees develop pinkish-tan, peeling bark that turns reddish-brown at maturity; larval food for butterflies (Compton tortoise shell, mourning cloak) and moths (polyphemus, rosy hook-tip)	Squirrels and birds eat fruit; small seedlings transplant best; leaf patterns vary on each tree (unlobed, mitten-shaped, trilobed) and display brilliant fall color; insects pollinate male and female flowers (on separate trees); larval food for spicebush swallowtail butterfly and moths (promethea, imperial, io); not winter hardy north of Missouri River	Birds take cover in branches at night, during winter; owls and hawks nest in branches; larval food for small pine elfin butterfly; not winter hardy north of Missouri River	Hummingbirds and insects feed on nectar and pollen of large, yellow flowers trimmed in orange; larval food for tiger swallowtail butterfly; one of the tallest native trees; named for tulip-silhouette leaf or shape of flower; not winter hardy north of Missouri River	Winged seeds eaten by finches and other songbirds; favorite larval food for tiger swallowtail butterfly; male and female flowers (on separate trees); brilliant mix of gold, orange and purple fall color

The Difference Between Shrubs and Trees

A shrub, bush and shrubbery are all small, woody plants that generally spread or bush out from the ground with multiple stems. A tree is a large, woody plant that usually grows from a single stem or trunk. Some trees, such as flowering dogwoods, hawthorns and redbuds, sometimes develop multiple stems and take on a bushy form, especially if cut or damaged when young. Some shrubs occasionally grow from a single stem. For the sake of simplicity, small trees and shrubs are both included under shrubs.

Understory Trees and Shrubs

After choosing a few large trees, fill in the understory with shorter native trees, shrubs and woodland wildflowers. Select native, early-blooming and shade-tolerant trees and shrubs. Excellent examples include serviceberry, redbud, flowering dogwood and pawpaw trees and shrubs such as spicebush, golden

Jim Rathert

currant and aromatic sumac. These early-blooming species flower before large deciduous trees leaf out and begin to reduce the amount of sunlight reaching the understory.

Many native, late-blooming shrubs and small woodland trees that flower after the tall trees leaf out get by on filtered sunlight. However, these species can flourish along the edge of the woods or where they receive more light. Hollies, hawthorns, red buckeye, viburnums, black-berries, blueberries and sumacs all increase flower and fruit production with more sun. The greater the flower and fruit production, the greater the wildlife benefit. In fact, most late-blooming and early-blooming shrubs and trees actually do better growing outside the forest in a yard, field or prairie environment where they get more sun. Because almost all of these woody plants grow better in full sun, look for more information in the next chapter on sun landscapes.

Jim Rathert

LEFT *Serviceberry, redbud, pawpaw and this flowering dogwood are examples of understory trees that bloom early. Dogwoods are slow-growing, but their delicate white flower-like bracts are worth the wait.* **ABOVE** *Redbuds, on the other hand, grow fairly fast and are hardy. This female evening grosbeak is perched on a redbud branch in full flower. A chart of shade-adapted, understory trees and shrubs appears on the next page.*

Understory Trees & Shrubs That Grow Well in Shade

This is a list of smaller trees and shrubs, 25 feet and shorter, that bloom in early spring, grow well in shade but also thrive in full sun. They all provide excellent wildlife food and cover. Keep in mind that soil described as dry generally is found on ridge tops, south- and west-facing slopes and drains quickly. Moist soil drains slowly and includes most urban soils and north- and east-facing slopes. Wet soils are low-lying and often water-saturated.

NAME	American Hazelnut *Corylus americana*	Downy Serviceberry *Amelanchier arborea*	Eastern Redbud *Cercis canadensis*	Flowering Dogwood *Cornus florida*	Fragrant Sumac *Rhus aromatica*
SIZE	8 ft. tall 8+ ft. wide	25 ft. tall 12 ft. wide	20 ft. tall 5 ft. wide	25 ft. tall 15 ft. wide	3-5 ft. tall 5-12 ft. wide
WHEN DOES IT FLOWER?	February-April	March-April	March-April	April-May	March-April
FLOWER COLOR	small, brown	white	pink and purple	yellow-green	yellow
UNIQUE OR ATTRACTIVE FEATURES?		bark, flowers	flowers	fall color	flowers, leaves, fall color
WHAT WILDLIFE COVER AND FOOD DOES IT PROVIDE?	general cover, clumps or thickets; butterfly/moth larval food, nuts	general cover; insect food, summer fruit, seeds	general cover; butterfly/moth larval food, insect food, seeds	butterfly/moth larval food, fall fruit for migrating birds	general cover, clumps or thickets; butterfly/moth larval food, insect food, summer fruit
GROWS IN WHAT KIND OF SOIL?	dry, moist	dry, moist	dry, moist	dry	dry, moist
COMMENTS	Early male flowers (catkins) food for grouse and deer; larger birds and mammals eat nuts; larval food for polyphemus moth; forms small, dense thickets by root suckers	Birds and mammals feed on berries; white flowers furnish early nectar and pollen for insects; one of the first trees in the forest to bloom; bark has shallow, vertical grooves	Flower clusters arise directly from branches and trunk; early nectar and pollen source for insects; a few birds and small mammals eat seeds; heart-shaped leaves larval food for Henry's elfin butterfly; flowers after service-berry and wild plum, before flowering dogwood	Important high-fat, red fruits for migrating songbirds, quail, turkey and mammals; larval food for spring azure butterfly and moths (friendly probole, buttercup); large, white, flower-like bracts surround small flowers; red to purple fall color; plant in shade or part shade; not winter hardy north of Missouri River	Hairy, red berries eaten by birds and mammals; flowers with early pollen for insects; larval food for red-banded hairstreak butterfly and regal moth; spreads by root suckers; leaves are aromatic when crushed; three-leaf pattern similar to poison ivy but distinguished by no stalk on middle leaflet; spreads by underground stems

Golden Currant *Ribes odoratum*	Missouri Gooseberry *Ribes missouriense*	Pawpaw *Asimina triloba*	Red Buckeye *Aesculus pavia*	Spicebush *Lindera benzoin*	Wild Plum *Prunus americana*
5 ft. tall 5 ft. wide	3 ft. tall 6 ft. wide	20 ft. tall 10 ft. wide	20 ft. tall 15 ft. wide	7 ft. tall 7 ft. wide	30 ft. tall 25 ft. wide
April-June	April-May	April-May	April-May	March-May	March-April
yellow	yellowish-white	maroon	red	yellow	white
			leaves	leaves, fall color	
general cover; butterfly/moth nectar, hummingbird nectar, summer fruit	general cover; butterfly/moth nectar, hummingbird nectar, summer fruit	clumps or thickets; butterfly/moth larval food, summer fruit	general cover; hummingbird nectar, nuts	general cover; butterfly/moth larval food, insect food, fall fruit for migrating birds	general cover, clumps or thickets; butterfly/moth nectar, butterfly/moth larval food, insect food, summer fruit
dry, moist	dry, moist	moist, wet	moist, wet	moist, wet	dry, moist
Small clusters of fragrant, tubular flowers nectar for hummingbirds and butterflies; berries eaten by birds and mammals; lacks spines	Small clusters of white flowers furnish nectar for hummingbirds and butterflies; larval food for gray comma butterfly; berries eaten by birds and mammals; thorny clumps provide cover	Only Midwest larval food for zebra swallowtail butterfly, larval food for pawpaw sphinx moth; ripe fruit tastes like banana, looks like a stubby banana, eaten by raccoons and opossums; forms thickets by underground stems; difficult to relocate due to long taproot; small seedlings transplant best; not winter hardy north of Missouri River	Tubular, red flowers are magnets for hummingbirds; flowering timed to return of hummingbirds; frost-resistant leaves emerge early in spring, leaflets attached in circular (palmate) pattern; tree named for large buckeye nuts; grows well in full sun; not winter hardy north of Missouri River	Glossy, bright-red fruits eaten by birds and mammals; primary larval food for spicebush swallowtail butterfly; fragrant flowers furnish early nectar and pollen for insects; leaves once used as spice, aromatic when crushed, turn bright yellow in fall	Fruit is primarily eaten by mammals (foxes, raccoons) and some larger birds; flowers furnish early pollen for insects; larval food for butterflies (hairstreaks, viceroys) and moths (cecropia, sphinxes); one of the first trees in the forest to bloom; excellent early nectar source for insects (spring azure—first native butterfly to emerge from overwintering pupae)

Dave Tylka

To Rake, or Not to Rake?

The ground in most Midwest forests is covered with a layer of tree leaves and other decaying plant material called duff. This duff is important to the forest ecosystem because as it decomposes, it releases nutrients into the ground that may be absorbed by the trees, shrubs, ferns and wildflowers. The richness of many forest soils results from the breakdown of duff over the years.

Sometimes before they can decompose, leaves may accumulate in low areas, tightly pack down and prevent wildflowers from emerging. If this occurs, rake the leaves up and shred with a mower or compost them. Since many woodland wildflowers, shrubs and trees favor a neutral to slightly acidic pH, the decomposing duff helps shade plants by contributing acidity to the soil. The duff also doubles as mulch, helping the forest plants conserve moisture. In general, take advantage of these natural benefits and do not rake the leaves in your shade landscape.

If the appearance of unraked leaves still bothers you, rake them up and compost them. After decomposition, spread the compost back out underneath your woodland plants as mulch. If windblown leaves from your shade landscape tend to migrate to unwanted areas, run over the leaves or duff with a mower to cut them up into smaller pieces. The smaller pieces are not blown around as easily by the wind and will decompose faster, especially if you have a mulching blade on your mower. To avoid scalping roots or plants, set your mower to the tallest setting.

Woodland Wildflowers

Most spring woodland wildflowers emerge from the forest floor and capture sunlight to bloom and fruit before the tree leaves shade the ground. Visually, a carpet of woodland spring wildflowers with a backdrop of flowering dogwoods has few equals in the Midwest. The first butterflies, bees, beetles and ants of spring depend upon the nectar and fruits produced by native wildflowers. In turn, the animals pollinate the flowers and distribute the seeds across the forest floor. Other small, ground-dwelling forest animals, such as box turtles and chipmunks, also take advantage of these food sources in the spring when few other plant foods are available.

Most woodland wildflowers require ample amounts of moisture to flower. During summer droughts, periodically water the soil to keep it moist. Newly planted wildflowers should be watered for the first four to six weeks after planting and only lightly mulched (about an inch thick) with well-decomposed and weed-free compost. After the wildflowers are established, you can gradually increase the amount of compost to about two to three inches.

Jim Rathert

LEFT *Wild sweet William is also called blue phlox. It grows to about 12 inches and pushes up through leafy ground.* **ABOVE** *Woodland wildflowers—such as the fire pink, wild geranium and blue-eyed Mary—are especially eye-catching when grouped together. A chart of recommended woodland wildflowers appears on the next page.*

Woodland Wildflowers for Shade Landscapes

This is a list of perennial and annual wildflowers that grow best in shade landscapes with rich, moist soils. They are used by wildlife as food. Keep in mind that soil described as dry generally is found on ridge tops, south- and west-facing slopes and drains quickly. Moist soil drains slowly and includes most urban soils and north- and east-facing slopes. Wet soils are low-lying and often water-saturated.

NAME	SIZE	WHEN DOES IT FLOWER?	FLOWER COLOR	WHAT WILDLIFE FOOD DOES IT PROVIDE?	GROWS IN WHAT KIND OF SOIL?	COMMENTS
American Bellflower or Tall Bellflower *Campanula americana*	36-60" tall	June-October	blue to lavender	insect food	moist	Annual plant reproduces by seed; flowers bloom along stem near top of tall plant; fall nectar source for forest insects; crab spiders rest on petals to capture and eat nectaring insects
Bloodroot *Sanguinaria canadensis*	4-8" tall	March-April	white	insect food	moist	Early-blooming, fragrant flower; nectar and pollen source for insects; unique, deeply cut leaves are attractive groundcover; reproduces by seeds and rhizomes; large, fleshy roots contain blood-like liquid used as homemade dye; ants aid seed dispersal
Bluebells *Mertensia virginica*	18-24" tall	April-May	blue, fading to pink	butterfly/moth nectar, insect food, hummingbird nectar	moist, wet	One-inch-long nodding, trumpet flowers furnish nectar and pollen for butterflies, hummingbirds, over-wintering queens of carpenter bees and bumblebees; reproduces by seeds and rhizomes; forms dense colonies in moist woods; foliage disappears after flowering; ants aid seed dispersal
Blue Phlox or Wild Sweet William *Phlox divaricata*	8-16" tall	April-June	blue to violet	butterfly/moth nectar, insect food, hummingbird nectar	moist	Showy flowers vary in color; good nectar source for butterflies and hummingbirds; leaves and flowers browsed by deer; grouse eat seed capsules
Celandine Poppy *Stylophorum diphyllum*	12-24" tall	April-May	yellow	butterfly/moth nectar, insect food	moist	Showy, four-petaled flower; nectar and pollen source for insects and butterflies; deeply-cut leaves last through summer in moist soils; seeds explode out of fuzzy capsules; ants aid seed dispersal
Columbine *Aquilegia canadensis*	20-30" tall	April-June	red and yellow	hummingbird nectar	dry, moist	Excellent nectar source for hummingbirds; larval food for columbine dusky wing butterfly; leaf miner insects feed on leaves and produce winding trails; long taproot makes transplanting difficult
Dwarf Crested Iris *Iris cristata*	6-8" tall	April-May	purple	insect food	moist	Showy flower with white or yellow fuzzy beard on dark purple petal; bees pollinate; forms flower colonies with creeping rhizomes; ants aid seed dispersal; also grows well in partial sun
False Solomon's Seal *Maianthemum racemosum*	24" tall	May-June	white	insect food, summer fruit	moist	Arching stems up to 3' produce clusters of star-like flowers at the end; red berries eaten by birds and small mammals
Golden Ragwort *Packera obovata* (formerly *Senecio obovatus*)	12-18" tall	April-June	yellow	butterfly/moth nectar, insect food	moist	Flower heads in umbrella-like cluster on stem above base leaves; nectar food for native bees; larval food for northern metalmark butterfly; leafy groundcover produced by creeping roots; adapted to deep soils at base of forest slopes
Horsemint or Bee Balm *Monarda bradburiana*	12-24" tall	April-June	lavender, white	butterfly/moth nectar, insect food, hummingbird nectar	dry, moist, grows well in acidic, nutrient-poor soils	Flowers form round clusters at top of square stems; nectar food for bees, butterflies and hummingbirds; adapted to nutrient-poor, acid soils in forest openings, glade borders; leaves minty when crushed

		JEWELWEEDS AND TOUCH-ME-NOTS					VIOLETS			
Jacob's Ladder *Polemonium reptans*	Jack-in-the-Pulpit *Arisaema atrorubens*	Spotted Jewelweed *Impatiens capensis*	Pale Jewelweed *Impatiens pallida*	Pussy Toes *Antennaria parlinii*	Solomon's Seal *Polygonatum commutatum*	Spring Beauty *Claytonia virginica*	Bird's Foot Violet *Viola pedata*	Blue Violet *Viola sororia*	Wild Geranium *Geranium maculatum*	Wild Ginger *Asarum canadense*
10-16" tall	10-18" tall	36-60" tall	36-60" tall	6-12" tall	24-36" tall	3-6" tall	2-5" tall	3-6" tall	10-18" tall	4-6" tall
April-June	April-June	May-October	May-October	April-June	May-June	February-May	April-June	March-June	April-June	April-May
blue	greenish-brown	orange	yellow	white with yellow or pink tint	white	pinkish-white	purple	bluish-purple	rose, lavender	maroon
insect food, butterfly/moth nectar	insect food, summer fruit, seeds	hummingbird nectar	hummingbird nectar	butterfly/moth larval food, insect food	insect food, summer fruit	butterfly/moth nectar, insect food	butterfly/moth larval food, insect food	butterfly/moth larval food, insect food	insect food	butterfly/moth larval food, insect food
moist	moist	moist, wet, grows well in acidic, nutrient-poor soils, tolerates clay soils	moist, wet, tolerates clay soils	dry, moist, grows well in acidic, nutrient-poor soils	moist	dry, moist, tolerates clay soils	dry, grows well in acidic, nutrient-poor soils	moist	moist	moist
Nectar and pollen source for bees and butterflies; crab spiders capture and eat nectaring insects from bell-like flowers; foliage disappears after flowering	Unusual flower-like structure has a hollow tube with a solid cylinder (Jack) partially covered with a curved hood; large leaves disappear in July or August; clusters of orange to red fruits on a stalk	Annual plant reproduces by seeds, sometimes forms dense colonies; shallow-rooted plant easy to pull; cornucopia-shaped flower is a hummingbird nectar magnet; seeds catapult away from parent plant; juice from stems relieves itching of stinging nettle, poison ivy and mosquito bites; prefers acidic soils	Annual plant reproduces by seeds, sometimes forms dense colonies; shallow-rooted plant easy to pull; cornucopia-shaped flower is a hummingbird nectar magnet; seeds catapult away from parent plant; juice from stems relieves itching of stinging nettle, poison ivy and mosquito bites; prefers alkaline limestone soils	Excellent nectar and pollen source for insects; male and female flowers on separate plants—males tinted with yellow, females tinted with pink; named for woolly flowers; mat of whitish hairs cover leaves and stems; attractive ground cover with underground runners; primary larval food for American painted lady butterfly; leaves eaten by mammals	Arching stem grows up to 4", small clusters of bell-shaped, drooping flowers along the stalk; blue fruits eaten by birds and small mammals	Early-blooming forest wildflower; nectar source for small bees and butterflies; easy to transplant by dividing small tubers after flowering; deer eat leaves and small mammals eat tubers; leaves disappear after flowering; ants aid seed dispersal	Flowers vary from lavender to purple; deeply cut leaves resemble bird's foot; larval food for fritillary butterflies; adapted to poor, dry openings in the forest; ants aid seed dispersal	Heart-shaped leaves remain green throughout growing season and form ground cover; nectar source for bees; larval food for fritillary butterflies; ants important in seed dispersal	Showy flower cluster atop stem furnishes good nectar and pollen for forest insects; long blooming period; seeds catapult away from parent plant; slowly spreads by rhizomes	Round, heart-shaped leaves dark green, covered with short, dense hairs for a velvety sheen; forms low-spreading ground-cover; ants aid seed dispersal

Wildflower Sources

To begin planting a wildflower landscape, there are many approaches—collecting seed from the wild, buying seeds or seedlings from wildlfower nurseries and trading seedlings with other wildlife landscapers. Digging up wildflowers on public lands and state highway right-of-ways is illegal in many states. Although collecting wildflower seeds for personal use is permitted along some state highway properties, the easiest way to add woodland wildflowers to your shade landscape is to buy native wildflower seeds or seedling plants as bare-rooted plants, in pots or in plugs. For a list of native plant nurseries, see page 174. You may also access a current list of Grow Native! retail nurseries on the Internet at www.conservation.state.mo.us/programs/grownative. Take care to purchase native plants only from reputable nurseries that can assure you their seeds and plants are grown in greenhouses and not collected from the wild.

Contact local native plant organizations, such as state native plant societies, for information about wildflower exchanges or plant sales. These organizations also conduct salvage operations where they rescue native plants before lands are bulldozed for development. A web search using the terms "organizations" and "native plants" will bring up hundreds of addresses.

Dave Tylka

Rocks, Mosses, Lichens and Ferns

Rocks are wonderful additions to any yard, offering both habitat diversity and artistic accent. Many species of wildlife seek refuge near or under rocks. The moist environment under flat rocks offers shelter for ground beetles, red-backed and slimy salamanders and an occasional small ring-necked, worm or garter snake. Many landscaping businesses sell various shapes and sizes of rocks; some even come already adorned with mosses and lichens.

Mosses are simple plants that lack modern plant structures like roots and flowers and are restricted to shady and moist environments. Many microscopic creatures live in mosses and several birds, such as tufted titmice, use moss in their nest construction. Some people encourage moss growth by dusting rough-textured rocks with powdered sulfur to ensure an acidic pH and then dowsing the rocks with nutrients—liquid fertilizer, beer or dairy products such as buttermilk. Most mosses tend to be soft and green, while most lichens are grayish, crusty and peely. Consisting of a unique combination of fungi and algae, lichens commonly grow on bare rocks and tree trunks. Warblers and hummingbirds use lichens for nesting materials.

Like mosses, ferns are simple plants that also prefer shaded, moist environments. With feathery leaf-like fronds, ferns are nice accent plants. Some mammals such as deer occasionally eat the young, unfurling fern fronds called fiddleheads. Some people find fiddleheads tasty, too. For more information about mosses and ferns, look into the reference books listed on page 173.

Collecting mosses, lichens and ferns on public lands is also illegal in many states. Many native fern species are commercially available from the same nurseries that specialize in wildflowers. If you collect mosses or lichens on private lands to re-plant on your property, practice basic conservation ethics. After obtaining the landowner's permission, take only small plugs or pieces and take them only from large, thriving populations. Please realize that mosses and lichens are slow-growing plants and probably have taken many years to grow.

Jim Rathert

Cliff White

LEFT *If your property is dotted with rocks that have been there a long time, they may already have colorful lichens growing on them. Many plant species also grow well among rocks.* **ABOVE, TOP** *Mosses and lichens, such as this reindeer lichen and British soldiers, add dashes of texture to native landscapes.* **ABOVE, BOTTOM** *Wild ginger, with its attractive heart-shaped leaves, is a nice cover around decks and patios. It emerges early in spring—when people are itching to be outside, too.*

sun landscapes

Chapter Five

*R*uby-throated hummingbirds, sulphur butterflies, bluebirds, goldfinches and other wildlife favorites are right at home in sun landscapes. The sun-loving wildflowers, grasses, shrubs, small trees and vines native to this region offer you a palette of colors and textures. Considering the many arrangements you can create, sun landscapes on your property are limited only by your imagination.

Although eight hours of sun is optimal, sun landscapes should receive a minimum of six hours of full sun a day during the growing season. If your shade and sun landscapes meet, remember the tallest plants usually win the competition for sun where these landscapes converge. In transition areas, consider stair-stepping plants from large trees to understory trees to shrubs to wildflowers. Physical borders such as fences, rock walls, patios and walkways can help fill the barren areas along transition zones. Although vines require periodic trimming, you can use them to decorate fences and rock walls.

Wildlife in the Sun

Sun landscapes not only provide beauty with diversity, but also habitat for a tremendous variety of wildlife. Flowers, seeds and fruits in full-sun landscapes attract many animal species that are plant-eaters—herbivores. Bees, beetles, butterflies and hummingbirds are attracted to flowers for energy-rich nectar and pollen. When wildlife visit the flowers for these foods, they also pollinate the flowers, which results in the production of seeds and fruits. Goldfinches, quail and sparrows eat grass and wildflower seeds, plus distribute undigested seed. Fruits from shrubs and trees are food for orioles, tanagers, thrushes, squirrels and raccoons, and more seeds found within the fruits are consequently distributed. Butterflies and birds rank high when it comes wildlife popularity, so Chapter Six covers specific details about their habitat needs.

Herbivores attract carnivores. Insect predators, such as dragonflies and praying mantises, feed on other insects. Everything from insects and spiders to frogs and mice become prey for swallows, flycatchers, wrens, shrikes, kestrels, harriers and other larger carnivores attracted to sun landscapes.

Shrubs and small trees growing in full sun attract fruit-eating birds and mammals. When selecting different species of shrubs and small trees for your property, key in on the size of the plant, but also to the season when it bears fruit. Because prairies are the most colorful and diverse of all the natural sun landscapes found in the Midwest, they are the focus for establishing a sun landscape.

Dave Tylka

CHAPTER COVER PAGE *There are many ways to arrange and border your native plantings. If you prefer a tidy appearance around your home, make use of fences, sidewalks, rocks, trellises and mulch.* **ABOVE** *Beetles are the most plentiful and, arguably, among the most beautiful of all invertebrates. This red milkweed beetle makes squeaking sounds by rubbing together rough areas on its thorax.*

Jim Rathert

Central Prairies

Using Missouri as a Midwest example, yearly rainfall amounts in the state increase as you travel from the northwest corner of Missouri to the southeast corner. Less rainfall favors grasses and wildflowers over trees. More than 200 years ago, prairies and savannas dominated the sun-rich landscape in the western and northern portions of Missouri. By definition, prairies are natural communities of drought-tolerant, sun-loving, native perennial grasses and wildflowers (often called forbs). Prairies are rich in species diversity—in some localities of Missouri, an acre of prairie can support more than 100 different plant species. Savannas are areas of transition between forests and prairies. They have prairie grasses and smatterings of large trees.

Prairies originally occurred on the flat and rolling plains of western and northern Missouri. Prairie-like communities called glades occur on some dry, south- and west-facing oak-hickory forest slopes, as well as in forest openings where there is a thin, rocky layer of soil that does not support tree growth. Savannas are basically prairies with scattered large trees, tolerant to fire. Walter Schroeder, prairie historian, estimates that 27 percent of Missouri was prairie in presettlement times; currently only one-half of one percent remains. Prairie landscapes of western and northern Missouri have become grass pastures, croplands, meadow and developments.

Native plants of the Midwest's prairies, glades and savannas all are adapted to full-sun situations and require the same site preparation. For ease of planning and planting, all of the grassland and wildflower communities are included under one category in this book—prairies. Prairie wildflowers and grasses, along with shrubs, small trees and vines, are the primary plant groups found in natural sun landscapes.

Visit Prairies for Ideas and Inspiration

Although species of wildflowers, grasses, shrubs and vines attractive to wildlife are listed here for your reference, you may also want to visit nearby public prairies at different times during the year, especially April through October. Not only are native prairie plants adapted to dry conditions, but also their growth and flowering take place the most during the warm months beginning in April. This growth period is why prairie grasses and wildflowers are referred to as warm-season plants. Warm-season species typically brown up earlier in the fall, around October. This is an excellent time to discover strange looking wildflower seed heads and bronze stalks of grass tipped with seeds.

During your prairie visit, take note of any plants that attract your attention or the attention of the local wildlife. Check out the distinctive seed heads on big bluestem or sideoats grama grass and observe the wildflowers that attract

"When I got to be 70, I thought, I'm going to take time to do what I really yearn to do, and that is work with native plants, wildflowers and trees, and encourage their use in the nation's landscape so they won't just be something of the past but will be passed on to our grandchildren."

*Lady Bird Johnson,
February, 1988*

LEFT *Take a day to visit a prairie at a state park or conservation area near your home. Many native plant enthusiasts will say that it was their first visit to a prairie in full bloom that turned them on to the joys of landscaping with natives. The Midwest is known for its prairies, and their diversity and color can be staggering.*

Jim Rathert

the most butterflies and hummingbirds. Look closely at the flower heads and see if any harbor tiny predators such as ambush bugs or crab spiders. To help identify plants, take along a field guide or camera. Make notes, too, and bring home ideas about your favorite features of these sun landscapes to copy on your property.

Keep in mind that, to some people, the brown plants may take on an untidy appearance and require explanation. If you decide to plant prairie species on your property, remember how seasonal variations will appear and then choose an appropriate location. On small properties where your neighbors live close by, you may want to inform them of your plans. Having a manicured, cool-season grass lawn (such as the native grasses Virginia wild rye and Canada wild rye) surrounding your prairie gives the appearance of control and neatness and provides a firebreak if you want to initiate a controlled burn of the prairie in the future.

Start Small With Prairies

After observing the beauty of a nearby prairie, you may be tempted to come home and convert your entire property. Establishing prairie from seed involves more labor than most conventional gardens, and it takes at least three years to accomplish. Whenever you break up the soil with a rake, shovel, tiller or tractor, weed seeds are brought up to the soil's surface to germinate and grow in the sun. Keeping down the population of aggressive, exotic weeds is the biggest challenge when establishing prairie.

ABOVE *Prairie grasses are remarkably colorful and change throughout the seasons.* **RIGHT** *Plains coreopsis is a good choice for beds because it doesn't take long to become established and usually will bloom the first year.*

Dave Tylka

To establish a small patch of prairie quickly in the spring, purchasing one- or two-year-old plants in pots or in bulk is probably your best choice. From the lists of grasses and wildflowers, choose about a 50:50 or 40:60 ratio of grasses to wildflowers and plant these on 12-inch centers. To keep down the weeds and conserve water, apply about a one-inch layer of finely textured mulch (not bark mulch) or compost around your plants. If plants begin to wilt during the first few weeks, water them with a sprinkler (enough to fill a container about three-quarters of an inch deep). Pull or carefully spray the weeds on a still day with a contact herbicide containing glyphosate (the brand names Roundup, Kleenup or Ranger). See "Eliminate Existing Plants, But Keep Soil Disturbance Minimal" on page 94 for more information about contact herbicides.

In more formal settings, smaller prairie wildflowers can be planted in borders, beds with linear or circular lines or centerpiece beds. For container gardens on decks or patios, you may want to choose some of the recommended small or medium-sized grasses and wildflowers. Plants taller than a couple of feet get lanky and generally are not suitable for pots. After some of these potted plants flower and lose some of their brilliance, move them to a less visible part of your property to overwinter. Before the next year's new growth appears, cut them back to achieve a fuller appearance.

If your plans include a prairie planting from seed, you may want to start off small. Even if you have a large backyard or several acres of land and prefer a non-formal approach to gardening, consider starting out with a prairie patch from 100 to 200 square feet. See how well your plant selection attracts butterflies and other wildlife. Then gauge the amount of time you devoted to preparing the site and

Ralph Waldo Emerson wrote, "What is a weed? A plant whose virtues have yet to be discovered." He is probably right, and landscaping with native plants affords people the chance to "discover" an abundance of new plants.

reducing weed growth before you go to a larger scale. If you decide to plant a large area from the start, you may want to get advice from a native plant nursery on your plans and plant choices, reducing the chance of a costly oversight. Because most soils contain many different species of dormant seeds and planting typically exposes many of the seeds, prairies are one of the most complex of all landscapes to establish.

Establishing Prairie Landscapes From Seed

When you consider time and expense, starting a prairie landscape from seed is the logical alternative for landscape areas more than 200 square feet. Keeping the population of aggressive, exotic weeds at bay is the biggest challenge when establishing prairie. There are even a few aggressive native plants that can cause problems. The more thoroughly you eradicate the existing plants and seeds from the site, the less time you spend weeding later.

The high plant and animal diversity found on native Midwest prairies is the result of thousands of years of evolution, periodic fires and several other factors. In perspective, establishing a prairie landscape in only three years is quite a feat, so patience is helpful in the process. The following seven steps outline the method of establishing a prairie landscape from seed that will probably work best for most situations in the central Midwest.

Choose the right location.

Match the right plants to the right locations.

Select the right balance of wildflowers and grasses.

RIGHT *Butterflyweed reaches three feet tall and blooms in many shades of orange to brick-red and sometimes yellow. The next few pages cover the steps it takes to establish a prairie landscape from seed.*

Jim Rathert

Eliminate existing plants, but keep soil
   disturbance minimal.
Estimate seeding rate and sow at the right time.
Watch for weeds and take action.
Maintain your prairie with periodic burning or mowing.

step 1: CHOOSE THE RIGHT LOCATION

Select a site that gets at least six, and preferably eight, daily hours of full, direct sun during the growing season. Trim overhanging tree limbs and cut back tall vegetation for better sun exposure. Most prairie plants listed do best in moist but well-drained sites where water does not pool after a good rain. Soils should not contain a high amount of clay. Seed that you broadcast on flat and gently sloping areas will stay on the site better than steep sloping areas. On moderate to steep slopes, a 50- to 75-percent covering of straw or fiber mat will help keep your seed from being washed away. This is especially challenging on heavy clay slopes where the soil is slick and the seeds and straw tend to slide downhill.

Some people prefer to locate prairie plantings a distance from their houses because of the prairie's informal appearance after the growing season. The golden stalks of grass tipped with seeds are attractive when viewed from your window, especially after the first snow blankets the ground. If you don't mind the informality and you like to observe the parade of flowers during the growing season, watch butterflies nectaring and see goldfinches pulling coneflower seeds, plant the prairie close to your house for easy viewing. Prairies make wonderful transitions between lawn and forest areas.

If you live in town, take time to visit with your neighbors about your prairie plantings to help avoid any misunderstandings. Having a well-mowed, cool-season grass lawn surrounding your prairie lends it the appearance of control and neatness. Some people border their prairies with rocks or split rail fences, while

81

Jim Rathert

others plant the edge with prairie dropseed grass for transition. Whether living or non-living, borders suggest that you are intentionally growing plants and containing them, rather than just letting an area grow up on its own. Many urban lawn ordinances allow vegetation within borders to be labeled as gardens. Keeping plant material receipts and recording the natural events in a journal adds credibility to your prairie.

step 2: MATCH THE RIGHT PLANTS TO THE RIGHT LOCATIONS

Choose the native wildflowers and grasses recommended that most appeal to you. If you want to specifically plant for birds and butterflies, be sure to read Chapter Six. Choose different plants for your property based upon site conditions such as the soil's clay content and moisture. Several of the design concepts from Chapter Three are appropriate here—select plants for a succession of blooms and plant tall vegetation in the back and short in the front.

Most native plant nurseries offer mixes based upon a specific site condition. Avoid buying seed mixes that are mass-produced and marketed in colorful seed envelopes and cans. These wildflower mixes typically are not seeds from or for a

Jim Rathert

ABOVE *A male goldfinch pauses on an equally golden wildflower, and a rose verbena serves up nectar to a species of clearwing moth.* **RIGHT** *An olive hairstreak, the only green butterfly in the Midwest, alights on a butterflyweed.*

specific region and do not contain native plant seeds. If getting something to bloom in your prairie during the first or second year is important and you are planting seeds, include Black-eyed Susan seed in your mixture.

Clay soils are typically poorly drained. They are very moist or wet in the spring, becoming very dry and hard in late summer. These contrasting conditions are extremely challenging for many plants.

On flat and gently sloping areas with a heavy clay content, there are two main options. The first is to improve the soil by adding four to six inches of topsoil or weed-free organic matter to the clay. When importing topsoil, you are potentially bringing in a new source of weed seeds with the soil, requiring more weed treatment later. Improving clay soils with topsoil or organic matter works well on small areas, but it is probably impractical on large areas.

The second option is to plant grasses and wildflowers adapted to clay soils. Clay-adapted prairie plants that attract wildlife are few, but if you are surrounded by heavy clay soils, this is probably your best option. Many newer subdivisions have had the

Jim Rathert

topsoil removed, leaving a thick layer of exposed clay. The one good side of this situation is that this ground is practically weed-free. If in doubt about your soil's clay content, call the county University Outreach and Extension Service for instructions on how to get soil analyzed. Adding fertilizer to the soil is not recommended for most native plants. In fact, adding fertilizer actually favors many fast-growing weeds.

step 3: SELECT THE RIGHT BALANCE OF WILDFLOWERS AND GRASSES

Strive for a mixture of both native perennial wildflowers and grasses. Perennials live more than two years and will grow back year after year if conditions are good for the species. In fact, some of these prairie plants have lived more than 50 years. Native plant nurseries usually sell seeds as well as one- or two-year-old plants that are adapted to our region. Native plant nurseries in the Midwest are listed on page 174.

A 50:50 or 40:60 ratio of grasses to wildflowers gives good ground coverage. Small bare patches invite weed growth. Weeds not only compete above the soil surface, but also below. Native grass roots grow large and help keep out weeds. Also, medium to tall wildflowers need

ABOVE *When planning your sun landscapes, choose a good mix of both flowers and grasses. Grasses produce seeds which are an important food source for many birds. A chart of recommended grasses appears on page 86.* **RIGHT** *A mix of tall, sun-loving wildflowers blooming in front of a house can be pleasantly surprising and welcoming, not to mention a boon for butterflies. Recommended sun-loving wildflowers appear in a chart on pages 88-93.*

Pat Whalen

grasses for physical support. For smaller prairie patches with wildflowers about three feet high, you may want to favor medium-height, native grasses that form bunches, such as side-oats grama, prairie dropseed and little bluestem. For medium- to large-sized prairies that support wildflowers taller than three feet, include taller grass species that reproduce by both seeds and rhizomes. Grasses that produce rhizomes can spread and colonize an area more quickly. They include big bluestem, Indian and switch grasses. Avoid aggressive varieties of Indian and switch grasses that have been developed for grazing such as Cheyenne Indian grass and cave-in-rock switch grass.

Native Grasses for Sun Landscapes

This is a list of grasses adapted to full sun landscapes (prairie, glade or savanna) and beneficial to native wildlife. Midwest mammals and butterfly caterpillars graze on grass blades, but the most valuable wildlife food from grasses is the seeds. Songbirds such as sparrows, ground-foraging birds such as quail, and small mammals such as ground squirrels eat the seeds. Grasses serve as physical supports for many prairie wildflowers and fill in bare spots in the soil to block out weeds. Most grasses are wind-pollinated.

Keep in mind that soil described as dry generally is found on ridge tops, south- and west-facing slopes and drains quickly. Moist soil drains slowly and includes most urban soils and north- and east-facing slopes. Wet soils are low-lying and often water-saturated.

NAME	Big Bluestem or Turkey Foot Bluestem *Andropogon gerardii*	Bottlebrush Grass *Elymus hystrix*	Broomsedge *Andropogon virginicus*	Buffalo Grass *Buchloe dactyloides*	Indian Grass *Sorghastrum nutans*	Little Bluestem *Schizachyrium scoparium*
SIZE	48-96" tall	24-48" tall	24-36" tall	4-8" tall	48-96" tall	24-48" tall
WHEN DO SEED STALKS FORM?	July-August	June	August-September	July-August	August	August
UNIQUE OR ATTRACTIVE FEATURES?	seed heads, stem color	seed heads	seed heads, fall color	seeds	seed heads, fall color	seed heads, stem color
WHAT WILDLIFE COVER AND FOOD DOES IT PROVIDE?	general cover, clumps or thickets; butterfly/moth larval food, seeds for birds and small mammals	general cover; seeds for birds and small mammals	general cover; seeds for birds and small mammals	seeds for birds and small mammals	general cover, clumps or thickets; seeds for birds and small mammals	general cover, clumps or thickets; seeds for birds and small mammals
GROWS IN WHAT KIND OF SOIL?	dry, moist, tolerates clay soils	dry, moist	dry; grows well in acidic, nutrient-poor soils	most tolerant of dry and compacted clay soils	dry, tolerates clay soils	dry, tolerates clay soils
COMMENTS	A tall, warm-season grass to plant among tall wildflowers; name turkey foot comes from seed head branching into three toes; blue to purple stems turn reddish-copper after frost; butterfly larval food (cobweb, arogos, dusted skippers)	Attractive seed head resembles a bottle brush; cool-season grass greens up early; tolerates some shade	Compact, warm-season grass that turns orange in fall, remains standing throughout the winter; sometimes called poverty grass, it thrives in poor soils; produces substance around roots to mildly inhibit shrub growth; similar to Elliot's broomsedge (*Andropogon elliotii*)	Short, warm-season grass with thin blades; along with blue grama grass, used as low-maintenance lawn in dry areas; extremely drought resistant; separate male and female plants; seeds produced in unique capsules only on female plants	Avoid aggressive varieties such as Cheyenne Indian grass; tall, warm-season grass to plant among tall wildflowers; produces attractive golden, plume-like seed head	Blue to purple stems turn reddish-brown after frost; attractive silvery-white seed heads; butterfly larval food for skippers; a shorter, warm-season, non-aggressive grass used to accent prairie wildflowers

Prairie Dropseed *Sporobolus heterolepis*	River Oats or Uniola Grass *Chasmanthium latifolium*	Sideoats Grama *Bouteloua curtipendula*	Silver Beard Grass *Andropogon ternarius*	Switchgrass *Panicum virgatum*	Virginia Wild Rye *Elymus virginicus*
12-24" tall	24-36" tall	12-30" tall	18-36" tall	36-72" tall	24-36" tall
August-September	July-August	July-August	August-September	July-August	June
seed heads	flattened seed heads	seed heads	seed heads, feathery, silver spikes on seeds	seed heads, fall color	seed heads
general cover; seeds for birds and small mammals	butterfly/moth larval food; seeds for birds and small mammals	seeds for birds and small mammals	general cover, clumps or thickets; seeds for birds and small mammals	general cover, clumps or thickets; seeds for birds and small mammals	seeds for birds and small mammals
dry	moist	dry	dry; adapted to nutrient-poor soils	dry, moist, tolerates clay soils	moist, tolerates clay soils
One of the most attractive warm-season grasses with arching, thin-bladed leaves and plume-like seed head; grows like a small version of the large ornamental fountain grass	Attractive warm-season grass with clusters of flattened seed heads, used in floral arrangements; tolerates some shade; butterfly larval food for some roadside skippers	Shorter, warm-season grass with thin blades; produces decorative oat-like seeds that hang distinctly to one side of the stem; a drought-resistant grass adapted to harsh conditions, common on glades; can be grown and mowed as a lawn	Attractive warm-season grass with silvery, beard-like clusters of seeds, persist throughout the winter; seed heads used in floral arrangements; tolerates poor soils but prefers sandy, well-drained soil	Avoid aggressive varieties such as Cave-in-Rock or Blackwell; tall, warm-season grass turns golden-yellow in fall	Cool-season grass, greens up early; dense seed head bends when mature; tolerates shade; excellent grass to plant as border around prairie, mow as firebreak; similar to Canada wild rye (*Elymus canadensis*)

Native Wildflowers for Sun Landscapes

Native wildflowers adapted to full sun are included here, especially prairie, glade or savanna plants beneficial to wildlife. Some full-sun water wildflowers are also included. Species are perennials, except for black-eyed Susan, Indian paintbrush and western wallflower. Keep in mind that soil described as dry generally is found on ridge tops, south- and west-facing slopes, and drains quickly. Moist soil drains slowly and includes most urban soils and north- and east-facing slopes. Wet soils are low-lying and often water-saturated.

	ASTERS		BLACK-EYED SUSANS OR RUDBECKIAS				BLAZING STARS
NAME	Aromatic Aster *Aster oblongifolius*	New England Aster *Aster novae-angliae*	Black-eyed Susan *Rudbeckia hirta*	Missouri Coneflower *Rudbeckia missouriensis*	Orange Coneflower *Rudbeckia fulgida*	Sweet Black-eyed Susan or Coneflower *Rudbeckia subtomentosa*	Eastern Blazing Star *Liatris scariosa*
SIZE	18-30" tall	48-72" tall	18-36" tall	12-30" tall	18-30" tall	36-60" tall	30-48" tall
WHEN DOES IT FLOWER?	August-October	August-October	June-July	July-September	July-September	August-September	August-September
FLOWER COLOR	blue or purple	purplish, but varies	yellow	yellow	orangish-yellow	yellow	purple
WHAT WILDLIFE FOOD DOES IT PROVIDE?	butterfly/moth nectar, butterfly/moth larval food, insect food	butterfly/moth nectar, butterfly/moth larval food, insect food	butterfly/moth nectar, insect food, seeds	butterfly/moth nectar, insect food, seeds	butterfly/moth nectar, insect food, seeds	butterfly/moth nectar, insect food, seeds	butterfly/moth nectar, insect food
GROWS IN WHAT KIND OF SOIL?	dry	moist tolerates clay soils	moist tolerates clay soils	dry	moist	moist tolerates clay soils	dry
COMMENTS	Shrub-like, fragrant aster a fair late nectar source for migrating monarchs and autumn insects; butterfly larval food for butterflies (silvery checkerspot, pearl crescent) and asteroid moth; sparrows, grouse and small mammals eat seeds; adapted to dry glades, savannas and prairies	Largest aster in the Midwest; dark purple color common; excellent late nectar source for migrating monarchs and autumn insects; butterfly larval food for butterflies (silvery checkerspot, pearl crescent) and asteroid moth; sparrows and small mammals eat seeds; adapted to moist areas in prairies and along streams	Annual wildflower grows on a variety of soils; nectar source for butterflies and insects; birds and small mammals eat seeds	Good nectar source for butterflies and insects; grows well in dry, hot landscape; well-adapted to hot, dry dolomite glades; birds and small mammals feed on seeds; look for crab spiders on flowers	Good nectar source for butterflies and insects; cultivars common; birds and small mammals eat seeds	Tall, bushy nectar source for butterflies and other insects; adapted to prairies; birds and small mammals eat seeds; flowers produce sweet, anise-like scent	Superior blazing star nectar source for butterflies, other insects and humming-birds; well-adapted to hot, dry dolomite glades

						CONEFLOWERS	
Prairie Blazing Star *Liatris pycnostachya*	Rough Blazing Star *Liatris aspera*	Blue or Great Blue Lobelia *Lobelia siphilitica*	Blue Sage *Salvia azurea*	Cardinal Flower *Lobelia cardinalis*	Compass Plant *Silphium laciniatum*	Glade Coneflower *Echinacea simulata*	Pale Purple Coneflower *Echinacea pallida*
30-54" tall	24-48" tall	12-30" tall	36-60" tall	24-48" tall	48-96" tall	24-36" tall	24-36" tall
July-September	August-September	September-October	August-September	August-September	July-August	June-July	June-July
purple	purple	blue	blue	crimson red	yellow	pink, purple	pink, purple
butterfly/moth nectar, insect food	butterfly/moth nectar, insect food	butterfly/moth nectar, insect food	insect food	hummingbird nectar	butterfly/moth larval food, insect food, seeds	butterfly/moth nectar, insect food, seeds	butterfly/moth nectar, insect food, seeds
moist tolerates clay soils	dry, moist	moist, wet	dry	moist, wet	dry, moist	dry, moist	dry, moist tolerates clay soils
Excellent nectar source for butterflies (especially swallowtails), insects and hummingbirds; tall flower spike blooms for long period; adapted to prairie	Excellent nectar source for butterflies, insects and hummingbirds; late flowering blazing star; tolerates dry glades and prairies	Nectar source for butterflies, insects and hummingbirds; related to cardinal flower, but blooms later; adapted to moist soils; look for crab spiders on flowers	Excellent nectar source for bees, butterflies and hummingbirds; bumblebee primary pollinator; adapted to dry glades and prairies	Superior nectar source for hummingbirds and cloudless sulphur butterfly; adapted to moist soils; common along streams, gravel bars	Fair nectar source for bees and insects; larval food for gorgone checkerspot butterfly and moths; seeds eaten by songbirds; deeply-cut basal leaves orient in a north-south direction, like a compass; adapted to prairies and dolomite glades	One of the best nectar sources for butterflies and insects; adapted to dry limestone and dolomite glades; finches eat seeds; look for crab spiders on flowers; yellow pollen distinguishes plant	One of the best nectar sources for butterflies and insects; adapted to dry limestone and dolomite glades; finches eat seeds; look for crab spiders on flowers; white pollen distinguishes plant

Native Wildflowers for Sun Landscapes (continued)

CONEFLOWERS *continued*

NAME	Purple Coneflower *Echinacea purpurea*	Yellow Coneflower *Echinacea paradoxa*	Copper iris *Iris fulva*	Culver's Root *Veronicastrum virginicum*	Fire Pink *Silene virginica*	Garden Phlox *Phlox paniculata*	Golden Alexander *Zizia aurea*
SIZE	28-48" tall	24-42" tall	18-30" tall	36-54" tall	8-20" tall	36-54" tall	18-30" tall
WHEN DOES IT FLOWER?	July-August	May-June	May-June	June-September	April-June	July-September	May-June
FLOWER COLOR	pink, purple	yellow	orangish red	white	scarlet red	pink	yellow
WHAT WILDLIFE FOOD DOES IT PROVIDE?	butterfly/moth nectar, insect food, seeds	butterfly/moth nectar, insect food, seeds	hummingbird nectar	butterfly/moth nectar, insect food	butterfly/moth nectar, insect food, hummingbird nectar	flowers butterfly/moth nectar, insect food, hummingbird nectar	butterfly/moth nectar, butterfly/moth larval food, insect food
GROWS IN WHAT KIND OF SOIL?	moist, tolerates clay soils	dry, moist, tolerates clay soils	wet	moist, tolerates clay soils	dry, grows well in acidic, nutrient-poor soils	moist	dry, moist, tolerates clay soils
COMMENTS	Good nectar source for butterflies and insects; finches eat seeds; adapted to prairies rather than glades; flowers later, longer than other coneflowers; prefers rich, moist soils	Good nectar source for butterflies and insects; finches eat seeds; adapted to dry limestone and dolomite glades	Only reddish iris in Midwest; good nectar source for hummingbirds; adapted to wet habitats	Candelabra-shaped flower spikes excellent nectar source for butterflies and insects; adapted to prairies	Excellent early-flowering nectar source for hummingbirds and some butterflies; adapted to dry, acidic soils (chert, sandstone, igneous rock base), along woodland edges and ledges; tolerates some shade	Tall, late-blooming perennial with pyramid-shaped flower clusters, nectar for hummingbirds, butterflies and insects; forms clumps; mildly aggressive	Flat-topped flower clusters good nectar source for butterflies and insects; important larval food for Missouri woodland swallowtail butterfly; adapted to glades, woodland edges and prairies

GOLDENRODS				MILKWEEDS			
Cliff Goldenrod *Solidago drummondi*	Showy Goldenrod *Solidago speciosa*	Indian Paintbrush *Castilleja coccinea*	Lanceleaf Coreopsis *Coreopsis lanceolata*	Butterflyweed *Asclepias tuberosa*	Common Milkweed *Asclepias syriaca*	Marsh or Swamp Milkweed *Asclepias incarnata*	Ohio Horsemint or Pagoda Plant *Blephilia ciliata*
18-30" tall	18-42" tall	8-18" tall	12-24" tall	18-36" tall	40-60" tall	40-60" tall	18-24" tall
September-October	September-October	April-June	May-June	June-August	June-August	June-August	May-August
yellow	yellow	red, but varies	yellow	orange	pink to lavender	pink to lavender	blue to pink to lavender
insect food, seeds	insect food, seeds	butterfly/moth nectar, hummingbird nectar	butterfly/moth nectar, insect food, seeds	butterfly/moth nectar, butterfly/moth larval food, insect food, seeds	butterfly/moth nectar, butterfly/moth larval food, insect food, seeds	butterfly/moth nectar, butterfly/moth larval food, insect food, seeds	butterfly/moth nectar, insect food, hummingbird nectar
dry	dry, moist	dry, moist	dry, tolerates clay soils	moist, dry	moist, tolerates clay soils	wet	dry, moist
Good nectar source for beetles, bees and flies active in fall; adapted to dolomite glades, ledges and cliffs (only goldenrod found on cliffs)	Good nectar source for beetles, bees and flies active in fall; very impressive Midwest goldenrod; adapted to prairies and meadows; slowly spreads by seeds, rhizomes	Color varies from red, orange to yellow; red and orange flowers attract hummingbirds; color comes from flower bracts, not tiny, greenish-yellow tubular flowers; hard-to-establish biennial best grown by scattering seed on open patches of soil; partial parasite on roots of other plants; adapted to glades and prairies	Both lanceleaf and large-flowered coreopsis (*Coreopsis grandiflora*, blooms about a month later) are good nectar sources for butterflies and small bees; adapted to dry glades by having small leaves, large flower heads	Excellent nectar source for butterflies (monarch, coral hairstreak); larval food for monarch caterpillars; slow-growing plant with showy flowers; challenging to transplant	Large, brawny plant appears rugged; provides many ecological interactions: flower clusters with abundance of nectar for pollinators (bumblebees, nocturnal moths, butterflies); flowers emit fragrance at night to guide moths; plants produce milky heart toxin, at least three insects are immune and gain protection from storing toxin in their bodies (monarch caterpillars, red-and-black milkweed bugs, milkweed beetles); look for ambushing crab spiders on flowers	Excellent nectar source for butterflies, especially monarchs; larval food for monarch caterpillars; adapted to wet habitats; grows in depressions where water pools after rain; needs mulch and water during dry summers	Excellent nectar source for butterflies and insects; non-aggressive mint; attractive flower arrangement of stacked round clusters; resembles a pagoda roof

Native Wildflowers for Sun Landscapes (continued)

NAME	Pickerel Weed *Pontederia cordata*	Prairie Dock *Silphium laciniatum*	Purple Beardtongue *Penstemon cobaea var. purpureus*	Purple Prairie Clover *Dalea purpurea*	Rattlesnake Master *Eryngium yuccifolium*	Rose Mallow *Hibiscus lasiocarpos*	Rose Turtlehead *Chelone obliqua*
SIZE	12-40" tall	36-96" tall	18-30" tall	18-24" tall	36-54" tall	42-72" tall	24-42" tall
WHEN DOES IT FLOWER?	June-October	July-September	May-June	June-August	July-August	August-September	September-October
FLOWER COLOR	violet-blue	yellow	purple	purple	white	white and deep red	rose pink
WHAT WILDLIFE FOOD DOES IT PROVIDE?	butterfly/moth nectar, insect food	butterfly/moth larval food, insect food, seeds	insect food, hummingbird nectar	butterfly/moth nectar, butterfly/moth larval food, insect food	butterfly/moth nectar, insect food	insect food, hummingbird nectar	butterfly/moth nectar, hummingbird nectar
GROWS IN WHAT KIND OF SOIL?	wet	dry, moist	dry	dry, tolerates clay soils	dry, moist, tolerates clay soils	wet	wet
COMMENTS	Attractive flower spike, arrow-shaped leaves; roots in water with stems emerging out of water; nectar source for many butterflies and insects; similar to other water plants with spreading rhizomes, forms large colonies; for small pools, plant in containers	Fair nectar source for bees and insects; larval food for gorgone checkerspot butterfly and moths; seeds eaten by songbirds; large flowers located at the top of tall (up to 8') almost leafless flower stalks arise from a clump of elephant ear-shaped basal leaves; adapted to prairies and dolomite glades	Large, tubular flowers are spectacular; good nectar source for large bees and hummingbirds; primarily pollinated by bumblebees; adapted to dolomite glades—keep site dry, mulch with gravel	Purple prairie and white prairie clover (*Dalea candida*) produce dense flowers on cylindrical flower heads, blooming from the bottom up; larval food for dogface sulphur butterfly; bees run around the head in circles collecting pollen—fun to observe	Unusual plant with round, white flowers, thick stems; basal leaves resemble yucca; excellent nectar source for butterflies, bumblebees and other insects; adapted to glades and prairies	Large, shrub-like and robust plant with one of the largest flowers (about 6") in the Midwest; deep-red center of white flower serves as hummingbird nectar guide	Rose and white turtlehead (*Chelone glabra*) excellent late-season nectar sources for hummingbirds and bumblebees

Rose Verbena *Glandularia canadensis*	Royal Catchfly *Silene regia*	Shining Blue Star *Amsonia illustris*	Water Willow *Justicia americana*	Western Wallflower *Erysimum capitatum*
6-12" tall	24-48" tall	24-36" tall	10-20" tall	12-36" tall
March-October	June-September	April-May	June-October	May-July
pink to magenta	scarlet red	blue	white with purple	yellow
butterfly/moth nectar, insect food	butterfly/moth nectar, insect food, hummingbird nectar	butterfly/moth nectar, butterfly/moth larval food, insect food, seeds	butterfly/moth nectar, insect food, seeds	butterfly/moth nectar, insect food
dry, moist	moist	moist	wet	dry
Early nectar for butterflies and insects; low, spreading plant adapted to open glades and prairies; long flowering period, but nectar production slows in hot months	Bright red, tubular flowers excellent summer nectar for hummingbirds and some butterflies; blooms most of summer; adapted to but uncommon on prairies, savannas and glades	Star-shaped flowers furnish nectar for butterflies; appears shrub-like with shiny, willow-like leaves; larval food for snowberry clearsing moth	Small, orchid-like flower excellent nectar source for insects and butterflies (skipper, swallowtails); spreading rhizomes form large colonies along shorelines; for small pools, plant in containers; use in streambank erosion control; territorial perches for black-winged damselfly	Showy biennial, excellent nectar source for butterflies and insects; reproduces by seeds, but does not re-seed well; adapted to glades

AGGRESSIVE AND UNDESIRABLE EXOTIC PLANT SPECIES

Many of the adaptable and aggressive exotic, sun-loving species listed below are prolific seed producers and spread by underground rhizomes.

autumn olive, *Elaeagnus umbellata*

bindweeds, *Calystegia spp.*

burning bush, *Euonymus alatus*

bush honeysuckles, *Lonicera morrowii and Lonicera maackii*

Caucasian bluestem, *Andropogon bladhii*

Canada thistle, *Cirsium arvense*

Chinese yam or cinnamon vine, *Dioscorea oppositifolia*

crown vetch, *Securigera varia*

common buckthorn, *Rhamnus cathartica*

common privet, *Ligustrum sinense*

common teasel, *Dipsacus laciniatus*

cut-leaved teasel, *Dipsacus fullonum*

daylilies, *Hemerocallis spp.*

field bindweed, *Convolvulus arvensis*

garlic mustard,* *Alliara petiolata*

Japanese honeysuckle, *Lonicera japonica*

Japanese knotweed, *Polygonum cuspidatum*

Johnson grass, *Sorghum halepense*

kudzu vine, *Pueraria lobata*

leafy spurge, *Euphorbia esula*

moneywort, *Lysimachia nummularia*

multiflora rose, *Rosa multiflora*

musk thistle, *Carduus nutans*

purple loosestrife,** *Lythrum salicaria*

Queen Anne's lace, *Daucus carota*

Russian olive, *Elaeagnus angustifolia*

sericea lespedeza, *Lespedeza cuneata*

spotted knapweed, *Centaurea maculosa*

sweet clover (white and yellow), *Melilotus alba and Melilotus officinalis*

tall fescue, *Festuca arundinacea*

water hyacinth,** *Eichhornia crassipes*

wild parsnip, *Pastinaca sativa*

winged euonymus, *Euonymus alatus*

wintercreeper, *Euonymus fortunei*

*invades shaded forest habitats
**invades wet habitats

step 4: ELIMINATE EXISTING PLANTS, BUT KEEP SOIL DISTURBANCE MINIMAL

Site preparation is essential. Remember, keeping down the population of aggressive, exotic weeds is your biggest challenge when establishing a prairie. The more thoroughly you eradicate the existing plants and seeds from the site, the less time you spend weeding later. Some lands have aggressive exotic plants so well established that they will not be converted to prairie landscapes without extensive treatments to kill the growing plants and rid the top layer of soil of weed seed. Sites with exotic legumes, such as crown vetch sericea lespedeza or birdsfoot trefoil are examples of aggressive plants. The goal is to end up with a bare soil surface free of most living plants and weed seeds.

There are three basic ways you can eliminate the existing vegetation: till the soil, solarize the soil (cover soil with black plastic sheeting or tarps) or directly spray a contact herbicide on growing plants. Contact herbicides containing the chemical glyphosate kill any green tissue that they come in contact with and neutralize or break down upon reaching the soil. Never spray on a windy day because the mist may drift and come into contact with non-targeted plants and kill them. The more times you till or apply herbicide, the more you eradicate unwanted plants. Each time you till, you also bring more weed seeds to the soil surface to germinate or sprout. If you have to disturb the soil, till only as deep as necessary to remove old roots. Many people still spray herbicide about three to six weeks after the final cultivation, eliminating the new weed seeds that have sprouted. Wait at least 10 days after spraying to plant your prairie seeds.

No-till methods of planting probably result in fewer weeds. One of the easiest landscapes to spray with herbicide and convert into prairie is a lawn, especially if it is relatively weed-free. A single herbicide application during the fall usually kills the grass. Afterward, mow the grass as close to the ground as possible. If there is not at least 20 percent bare ground for seed-soil contact, slightly scalp the ground with a weed whip. The more weed-free an area is, the less treatment is required.

If your potential prairie site has a weed problem, consider not tilling the soil and spraying several times or solarizing the site for the entire growing season. The more times you treat the area, the more undesirable plants you will eliminate. If your site has an abundance of undesirable plants, you may have to spend an entire year eliminating weeds. Johnson grass, crown vetch, tall goldenrod and most other undesirables not only produce tens of thousands of seeds, but also spread by rhizomes and are perennials. With survival adaptations like that, some perennial weeds are almost impossible to eliminate with one or two treatments of herbicide.

step 5: ESTIMATE SEEDING RATE AND SOW AT THE RIGHT TIME

If you choose your own seed mixture, use the 50:50 or 60:40 ratio of wildflowers to grasses to get good ground coverage. Allow for about 10 pounds of clean or pure live seed mix to cover an acre of prepared ground. Increase the rate by 50 percent or use about 15 pounds of mix if the seeds are not cleaned (seeds with chaff or husks still attached). For small prairies, an ounce of pure live seed mix (with average-sized wildflowers and grasses) covers about 250 square feet of ground. Don't forget, if you need something to bloom in your prairie during the first or second year, include some Black-eyed Susans.

Mix five parts of vermiculite, finely ground old sawdust or millorganite to one part prairie seeds to increase the bulk so you can distribute the seed more evenly. For smaller areas, hand broadcast the seeds or use a hand-crank cyclone spreader to spread the seeds over the soil surface if all the seeds are about the same size. For larger areas, you may want to use a tractor and a drill for planting native seeds. Chapter Eight includes suggestions on planting prairie seeds on larger properties. For good seed coverage on the site and to avoid holes in your coverage, divide the seed mixture in half. With the first half of your seed, spread it by walking in straight lines up and down your site. Spread the second half by walking in lines perpendicular to your first lines.

If you want to learn to identify young wildflowers and grasses in your planting, sow small amounts of prairie seed in sterilized soil off to the side of your planting or in a pot for comparison. You can either plant it at the same time you sow your prairie or store it in a sealed plastic bag with moist sand until March and then plant it. As prairie seedlings get bigger, the differences become more noticeable.

POTENTIALLY AGGRESSIVE NATIVE PLANT SPECIES

When establishing sun landscapes, avoid planting and reduce the populations of the following native species that can potentially dominate a new home prairie or garden landscape.

common sunflower, *Helianthus annuus*
horseweed, *Conyza canadensis*
joe-pye weed, *Eupatorium purpureum*
reed canary grass,** *Phalaris arundinacea*
sesbania,** *Sesbania exaltata*
sawtooth sunflower, *Helianthus grosseserratus*
slender mountain mint, *Pycnanthemum tenuifolium*
tall coreopsis, *Coreopsis tripteris*
tall goldenrod, *Solidago altissima*
tick trefoil, *Desmodium perplexum*
white heath aster, *Aster pilosis*
wild lettuce, *Lactuca canadensis*
wild potato vine, *Ipomoea pandurata*
yarrow, *Achillea millefolium*

**invades wet habitats*

Paul Childress

Native wildflowers and grasses are adapted to the Midwest and, in order for native seeds to germinate well, they should be exposed to winter weather conditions to help break or weaken the seed coats and emerge from dormancy. Cold, moist winter conditions and freeze-thaw cycles also help the seeds work into the soil for optimal seed-soil contact. Native prairie wildflowers are best planted from late November through early January. There is not a consensus on the best time to plant native warm-season grasses. If the mixture includes wildflowers, go with the November to January period for a prairie seed mix.

To spread the seed evenly, sow only on still days. Gusty winds play havoc with seed distribution. On moderate to steep slopes, a 50- to 75-percent covering of straw or fiber mat will keep your seed from being washed away. If you cover more than 50 percent of the bare ground with straw or fiber, the wildflowers' germination rate starts to diminish. On slick, steep slopes, you may need to use 75 percent cover to hold the seeds in place, so try to seek a balance. After the prairie seeds sprout, the vulnerable, young seedlings need adequate rain. If the seedlings start to wilt during the first six to eight weeks, water them immediately. If a drought hits right after sprouting and they begin to wilt, give them about a full inch of water once a week. If wilting continues, increase the amount. After the seedlings are eight weeks old, they are fairly well established and will tolerate most weather that comes along.

ABOVE *For seeding larger areas, you may want to rent or borrow a hand-crank seed spreader.* **RIGHT** *There are several kinds of beautiful goldenrods in the family Asteraceae. Goldenrods are often blamed for causing hayfever, yet the wind-blown pollens of ragweeds are the real culprits. Goldenrods are pollinated by bees, fall wasps and beetles, not wind.*

Jim Rathert

step 6: **WATCH FOR WEEDS AND TAKE ACTION**

During the first year or two, most energy produced by the prairie wildflowers and grasses goes into root development. Most prairie wildflowers grown from seed do not flower until the third year, so be patient. If a thick growth of weeds reaches a height of eight to 12 inches during the first year, mow everything back to four to six inches high. If you allow the weeds to get tall, they will produce not only weed seeds, but they will shade out prairie plants that are still growing good roots. Repeat weed cutting as necessary throughout the first year.

If the weeds become dense and grow 10 to 12 inches tall during the second year, mow everything back to six to eight inches tall. Should weeds dominate in the third and fourth years, you may have to start over from the beginning. To rig your lawnmower to cut four to eight inches off of the ground, you may have to purchase big wheels and raise the mowing deck. If you only have a small prairie, you can easily cut weeds with a string trimmer.

The key is to distinguish weeds from native prairie plants. Use pictures in field guides or compare the unknown plants to your sample plantings in sterile soil. If you still have doubts about your plant identification, take a few plant samples in a plastic bag or photographs of the plants to a nursery or nature center to get help in identifying young plants. If you can identify weeds during the first two years, they can be pulled, dug or spot-sprayed with a contact herbicide. The pulling action may disturb young wildflowers and grasses growing alongside and this disturbance may bring more weed seeds to the surface to sprout. As your prairie matures, take notice of what plants are becoming abundant and learn to recognize the desirable species from undesirable ones.

Most important, never let a weed or aggressive native plant produce seeds. If the seeds drop to the ground and sprout, this can compound your problems. At the very least, clip off the flower heads and discard them where they won't threaten native communities. It takes much less energy to control undesirable plants when you catch them early rather than if you wait until they are well established and then try to eliminate them.

During the winter, if you see small holes in the ground or slightly raised ground around your plants, you may have voles or field mice feeding on your new plants. If this happens, cut the vegetation short to expose the rodents more to predators.

Tom Troughton

step 7: MAINTAIN YOUR PRAIRIE WITH PERIODIC BURNING OR MOWING

In the fall of the third year when all the native plants have turned brown, carefully burn your prairie to stimulate native plant growth and keep out woody growth. If your prairie is greater than a few hundred square feet, you may want to burn only half of it at a time. Many beneficial prairie insects and other small animals overwinter in the brown grass and dried wildflower materials. If you burn your entire prairie all at once, you may lose wildlife populations and not have any nearby source of immigration. On larger stands of prairie, start off by burning portions of your prairie every other year; watch how your native plants respond and adjust your maintenance accordingly.

Burning exposes some of the soil to the sun and allows it to dry out and warm up better for next year's growing season. A good resource for conducting a controlled burn is *Planning and Conducting Prescribed Burns in Missouri*, a pamphlet available from the Missouri Department of Conservation. Other states' conservation agencies produce similar publications. Check with your local fire department for burn permits and procedures.

If burning is prohibited, mow close to the ground and rake off large pieces of vegetation instead of burning. Raking also allows the soil to warm and helps trigger the growth of native, warm-season grasses and wildflowers.

Jim Rathert

Shrubs and Small Trees

Grouping shrubs and small trees together is an excellent way to furnish fruits, berries and seeds to birds and mammals, as well as to provide cover. Small woody plants also serve as a linear transition zone between tall forest environments and shorter plantings, such as prairies or lawns. Although some of these species will grow under a forest canopy, they flower and produce more fruit in

LEFT *Fire was a natural and essential part of the prairie landscape before European settlement. Today, conservation agencies often set prescribed fires to public prairie lands to maintain and stimulate their growth. Depending on the size of your prairie landscape, you may want to burn it periodically, too. Always seek advice from your local conservation office or fire department before you burn.* **ABOVE** *The small nutlets found on buttonbush shrubs are eaten by at least 25 species of birds, especially water birds. It is also the best shrub nectar source for butterflies.*

the full sun. Native trees and shrubs that grow up to 30 feet tall are divided into two lists in this chapter—those that have an average size between 10 and 30 feet and beneficial shrubs that average 10 feet or less.

Jim Rathert

Three Fruit Categories

Not only are height and width important when selecting small trees and shrubs, but fruiting time and the type of fruit are also significant. Fruiting is key if you want to furnish natural foods to both nesting summer birds and migrating birds. Fruiting is equally essential to plants. Many native plants produce seeds surrounded by fleshy and juicy fruits, designed to attract native wildlife. Birds and mammals eat these fruits and later regurgitate or defecate seeds some distance away from the parent plant. New plants will grow from these seeds in a location away from the parent plant and in an area with less competition, or so the theory goes. Plants perpetuate themselves in this way.

Fruiting is divided into three broad categories, based upon which season the fruits and seeds are produced, their nutritional make-up and the length of time they remain on the plants. To attract the greatest diversity of birds and mammals to your property at various seasons, select fruiting shrubs and trees from each of the following three categories. Each category benefits a general group of animals.

Jim Rathert

SUMMER FRUITS

Shrubs and trees that fruit in the summer produce high-sugar fruits and are grouped as summer fruits. Summer fruits typically benefit both mammals and summer nesting birds.

FALL FRUITS

Native plants that fruit in the early fall produce high-fat and low-sugar fruits and are labeled fall fruits. Fall fruits are especially important to migrating birds.

WINTER FRUITS

Other fruiting shrubs and trees bear fruit in mid- to late fall. Most of these native plants develop low-fat and low-sugar fruits that persist well into the cold weather and are categorized as winter fruits. Mammals and winter bird residents benefit from winter fruits.

Please refer to Chapter Six, pages 128-135, to discover which native plant species will attract birds and mammals throughout various seasons.

LEFT *Many birds depend on the fruits and nuts of plants to survive. This northern mockingbird has sought out the seeds of a deciduous holly, also called possumhaw. The seeds stay on the branches into winter.*
ABOVE *Because most leaves are gone from trees in the winter and the branches are left unobscured, the winter season is a good time to birdwatch. Eastern bluebirds are a Midwest favorite and Missouri's state bird.*

Small Trees & Large Shrubs Adapted to Full Sun

This is a list of small trees and larger shrubs, 10 to 30 feet in height, that are adapted to full sun and highly beneficial to a wide array of Midwest wildlife. Keep in mind that soil described as dry generally is found on ridge tops, south- and west-facing slopes and drains quickly. Moist soil drains slowly and includes most urban soils and north- and east-facing slopes. Wet soils are low-lying and often water-saturated.

DOGWOODS

NAME	Chokecherry *Prunus virginiana*	Flowering Dogwood *Cornus florida*	Roughleaf Dogwood *Cornus drummondii*	Downy Serviceberry *Amelanchier arborea*	Eastern Redbud *Cercis canadensis*	Eastern Red Cedar *Juniperus virginiana*
SIZE	20 ft. tall 15 ft. wide	25 ft. tall 15 ft. wide	15 ft. tall 12+ ft. wide	25 ft. tall 12 ft. wide	20 ft. tall 15 ft. wide	25 ft. tall 10 ft. wide
WHEN DOES IT FLOWER?	April-May	April-May	May-June	March-April	March-April	
FLOWER COLOR	white	yellow-green	white	white	pink, purple	
UNIQUE OR ATTRACTIVE FEATURES	flowers	flowers, fall color	flowers, fall color	bark, flowers	flowers	
WHAT WILDLIFE COVER & FOOD DOES IT PROVIDE?	general cover; butterfly/moth nectar, butterfly/moth larval food, insect food, summer fruit	butterfly/moth larval food, fall fruit for migrating birds	general cover, clumps or thickets; butterfly/moth larval food, insect food, summer fruit	general cover; insect food, summer fruit,	general cover; butterfly/moth larval food, insect food, seeds	general cover, clumps or thickets, evergreen; butterfly/moth larval food, winter fruit
GROWS IN WHAT KIND OF SOIL?	dry	dry	dry, moist, tolerates clay soils	dry, moist	dry, moist	dry, moist
COMMENTS	Songbirds and chipmunks relish fruits, disperse seeds; larval food for tiger swallowtail butterfly and moths (blind-eyed, wild cherry sphinxes); excellent shade tolerance	Important high-fat, red fruits for migrating songbirds, quail, turkey and mammals; larval food for spring azure butterfly and moths (friendly probole, buttercup); large, white, flower-like bracts surround small flowers; red to purple fall color; plant in shade or part shade; not winter hardy north of Missouri River	Variety of songbirds, woodpeckers and mammals eat white berries; flat-topped flower clusters furnish nectar and pollen for insects; larval food for moths; songbird nesting cover; hardy; forms multi-stemmed thickets	Birds and mammals feed on berries; white flowers furnish early nectar and pollen for insects; one of the first trees in the forest to bloom; bark has shallow, vertical grooves	Flower clusters arise directly from branches and trunk; early nectar and pollen source for insects; a few birds and small mammals eat seeds; heart-shaped leaves larval food for Henry's elfin butterfly; flowers after serviceberry and wild plum, before flowering dogwood	Dense branches, the best winter roost for birds in the Midwest, especially at night; doves and other birds nest in small branches; blue fruit (fleshy cone) an important winter food for mammals and birds (cedar waxwings returning early in the spring); larval food for olive hairstreak butterfly (male is the only green Midwest butterfly); adapted to dry glades; dense visual screen or windbreak; if planted near hawthorn, crabapple and serviceberry, leaf diseases possible

HAWTHORNS				HOLLIES	
Cockspur Hawthorn *Crataegus crus-galli*	Downy Hawthorn *Crataegus mollis*	Green Hawthorn *Crataegus viridis*	Washington Hawthorn *Crataegus phaenopyrum*	American Holly *Ilex opaca*	Deciduous Holly or Possumhaw *ilex decidua*
18 ft. tall 20 ft. wide	30 ft. tall 25 ft. wide	25 ft. tall 15 ft. wide	20 ft. tall 20 ft. wide	30 ft. tall 20 ft. wide	16 ft. tall 16 ft. wide
May-June	April-May	May-June	May-June	May-June	April-May
white	white	white	white	small, white	small, white
flowers	flowers	flowers, bark	flowers	leaves	
general cover, clumps or thickets; butterfly/moth nectar, insect food, winter fruit	general cover, clumps or thickets; butterfly/moth nectar, insect food, winter fruit	general cover, clumps or thickets; butterfly/moth nectar, insect food, winter fruit	general cover, clumps or thickets; butterfly/moth nectar, insect food, winter fruit	general cover, evergreen; insect food, winter fruit	general cover; winter fruit, insect food
dry	dry	dry, moist, wet	dry	dry, moist	dry, moist, wet, tolerates clay soils
Birds and mammals eat the red fruits, persist into winter; small, dense and thorny branches are excellent bird nesting, roosting cover; pollen and nectar for butterflies and insects; longest thorns of any haws (3-4"); nearby cedars may cause leaf diseases	Birds and mammals eat the red fruits, persist into winter; small, dense and thorny branches are excellent bird nesting, roosting cover; pollen and nectar for butterflies and insects; long thorns (2"); nearby cedars may cause leaf diseases	Birds and mammals eat the red fruits, persist into winter; small, dense and thorny branches are excellent bird nesting, roosting cover; pollen and nectar for butterflies and insects; thin, greenish bark flakes off to reveal reddish inner bark; long thorns (1-2"); resists leaf diseases better than most haws	Birds and mammals eat the red fruits, persist into winter; small, dense and thorny branches are excellent bird nesting, roosting cover; pollen and nectar for butterflies and insects; long thorns (1-2"); resists leaf diseases better than most haws	Songbirds eat red berries after first hard frost; bees pollinate male and female flowers (on separate trees); stiff, evergreen and prickly leaves; winter and nesting cover for songbirds; leaves and berries collected for winter floral arrangements; grows slowly; not winter hardy north of Missouri River	Orange to red berries winter food for songbirds, quail and mammals (opossums); bees pollinate male and female flowers (on separate plants)

Small Trees & Large Shrubs Adapted to Full Sun (continued)

HOLLIES *continued*

NAME	Winterberry *Ilex verticillata*	Hop Tree or Wafer-ash *Ptelea trifoliata*	Pawpaw *Asimina triloba*	Prairie Crabapple *Malus ioensis*	Prickly-ash *Zanthoxylum americanum*	Red Buckeye *Aesculus pavia*
SIZE	12 ft. tall 10 ft. wide	18 ft. tall 15 ft. wide	20 ft. tall 10 ft. wide	20 ft. tall 15 ft. wide	12 ft. tall 10+ ft. wide	20 ft. tall 15 ft. wide
WHEN DOES IT FLOWER?	April-May	April-June	April-May	April-May	April-May	April-May
FLOWER COLOR	small, white	small, white	maroon	pink to white flowers	small, green and yellow	red
UNIQUE OR ATTRACTIVE FEATURES						flowers, leaves
WHAT WILDLIFE COVER & FOOD DOES IT PROVIDE?	general cover; winter fruit, insect food	general cover; butterfly/moth larval food, insect food, seeds	clumps or thickets; butterfly/moth larval food, summer fruit, seeds	general cover; butterfly/moth larval food, summer fruit	general cover, clumps or thickets; butterfly/moth larval food, insect food, summer fruit, seeds	general cover; hummingbird nectar, seeds
GROWS IN WHAT KIND OF SOIL?	moist, wet	dry, moist, tolerates clay soils	moist, wet	dry, moist	dry, moist	moist, wet
COMMENTS	Orange to red berries winter food for songbirds, quail, grouse and small mammals; bees pollinate male and female flowers (on separate plants)	Greenish-white, fragrant flowers with nectar for bees and insects; larval food for tiger swallowtail, one of two main larval foods for giant swallow-tails; papery, winged fruits	Only Midwest larval food for zebra swallowtail butterfly, larval food for pawpaw sphinx moth; ripe fruit tastes like banana, looks like a stubby banana, eaten by raccoons and opossums; forms thickets by underground stems; difficult to relocate due to long taproot; small seedlings transplant best; not winter hardy north of Missouri River	Mammals and ground-feeding birds eat apples; beautiful flowers furnish pollen for insects; larval food for butterflies (tiger swallowtail, red-spotted purple) and moths (short-lined chocolate moth); susceptible to leaf diseases; nearby cedars may cause leaf diseases	Fruit eaten by birds; flowers furnish nectar for bees; larval food for butterflies (tiger swallowtail, one of two main foods for giant swallowtail); forms thickets with underground stems; small spines found along branches; also called toothache-tree, fruits have numbing effect	Tubular, red flowers are magnets for humming-birds; flowering timed to return of hummingbirds; frost-resistant leaves emerge early in spring, leaflets attached in circular (palmate) pattern; tree named for large buckeye nuts; grows well in full sun; not winter hardy north of Missouri River

VIBURNUMS

Blackhaw *Viburnum prunifolium*	Nannyberry Viburnum *Viburnum lentago*	Rusty Blackhaw *Viburnum rufidulum*	Shining Sumac *Rhus copallina*	Wild Plum *Prunus americana*
30 ft. tall 20 ft. wide	30 ft. tall 25 ft. wide	15 ft. tall 10 ft. wide	20 ft. tall 25 ft. wide	30 ft. tall 25 ft. wide
April-May	May-June	April-May	May-July	March-April
white	white	white	white	white
flowers, fall color	flowers, fall color	flowers, fall color	leaves, fall color	flowers
general cover; winter fruit, butterfly/moth nectar, butterfly/moth larval food, insect food, seeds	general cover; winter fruit, butterfly/moth nectar, butterfly/moth larval food, insect food, seeds	general cover; winter fruit, butterfly/moth nectar, butterfly/moth larval food, insect food, seeds	general cover, clumps or thickets; butterfly/moth nectar, butterfly/moth larval food, insect food, seeds	general cover, clumps or thickets; butterfly/moth nectar, butterfly/moth larval food, insect food, summer fruit
dry, moist	moist	dry, moist	dry, moist, grows well in acidic, nutrient-poor soils	dry, moist
Fruits eaten by birds and mammals; butterflies and insects gather nectar and pollen from flower clusters; larval food for moths (hummingbird clearwing, rosy hook-tip); purplish-red fall color	Fruits eaten by birds and mammals; butterflies and insects gather nectar and pollen from flowers; larval food for moths (hummingbird clearwing, rosy hook-tip); susceptible to powdery mildew	Fruits eaten by birds and mammals; butterflies and insects gather nectar and pollen from flowers; larval food for moths (hummingbird clearwing, rosy hook-tip); transplants well; not winter hardy north of Missouri River	Compact cluster of seeds eaten by birds and mammals; good summer nectar and pollen source for insects; larval food for red-banded hairstreak butterfly and regal moth; scarlet red fall color; leaves winged; spreads by underground stems	Fruit is eaten primarily by mammals (foxes, raccoons) and some larger birds; flowers furnish early pollen for insects; larval food for butterflies (hairstreaks, viceroys) and moths (cecropia, sphinxes); one of the first trees in the forest to bloom; excellent early nectar source for insects (spring azure— first native butterfly to emerge from overwintering pupae)

Small & Medium Shrubs Adapted to Full Sun

This is a list of shrubs, 10 feet tall or shorter, that are adapted to full sun and highly beneficial to Midwest wildlife. Keep in mind that soil described as dry generally is found on ridge tops, south- and west-facing slopes and drains quickly. Moist soil drains slowly and includes most urban soils and north- and east-facing slopes. Wet soils are low-lying and often water-saturated.

				BLUEBERRIES		
NAME	American Hazelnut *Corylus americana*	Beautyberry *Callicarpa americana*	Blackberries, Dewberries and Raspberries *Rubus spp.*	Deerberry or Highbush Huckleberry *Vaccinium stamineum*	Farkleberry or Highbush Blueberry *Vaccinium arboreum*	Lowbush Blueberry *Vaccinium pallidum*
SIZE	8 ft. tall 8+ ft. wide	4 ft. tall 4 ft. wide	3-6 ft. tall 5+ ft. wide	4-5 ft. tall 4-5 ft. wide	10 ft. tall 10 ft. wide	2 ft. tall 5+ ft. wide
WHEN DOES IT FLOWER?	February-April	June-August	April-June	April-June	May-June	April-May
FLOWER COLOR	small, brown	rosy-violet	white	pink, white	pink, white	pink, white
UNIQUE OR ATTRACTIVE FEATURES				flowers	flowers	flowers
WHAT WILDLIFE COVER & FOOD DOES IT PROVIDE?	general cover, clumps or thickets; butterfly/moth larval food	butterfly/moth nectar, hummingbird nectar, winter fruit	general cover, clumps or thickets; insect food, summer fruit	general cover; butterfly/moth larval food, insect food, summer fruit	general cover; butterfly/moth larval food, insect food, summer fruit	general cover; butterfly/moth larval food, insect food, summer fruit
GROWS IN WHAT KIND OF SOIL?	dry, moist	dry, moist	dry, moist	dry, grows well in acidic, nutrient-poor soils	dry, grows well in acidic, nutrient-poor soils	dry, grows well in acidic, nutrient-poor soils
COMMENTS	Early male flowers (catkins) food for grouse and deer; larger birds and mammals eat nuts; larval food for polyphemus moth; forms small, dense thickets by root suckers	Unusual-colored (rosy-violet) fruits winter food for birds, especially bluebirds; tubular flowers nectar for butterflies and hummingbirds; plant may die back to ground during winter; not winter hardy north of Missouri River	High-sugar, fleshy fruits excellent for summer resident birds and mammals; excellent nectar and pollen source for insects; prickly brambles are cover for birds and small mammals; stems flower second year, do not cut back after first year; some species spread quickly	Many mammals and summer resident birds "eat fruits; insects gather nectar and pollen from flowers; larval food for Henry's elfin butterfly "and yellow-washed metarranthis moth; not winter hardy north of Missouri River	Fruits larger than deerberry and lowbush blueberries but dry, mealy texture; eaten by some mammal and summer resident birds; insects gather nectar and pollen from flowers; larval food for Henry's elfin butterfly and yellow-washed metarranthis moth; lichens grow on flaky bark; leathery leaves may persist throughout winter; not winter hardy north of Missouri River	Fruits ripen over a longer period than deerberry or farkleberry, eaten by several mammals and summer birds; insects gather nectar and pollen from flowers; larval food for Henry's elfin butterfly and yellow-washed metarranthis moth; may form colonies; not winter hardy north of Missouri River

DOGWOODS

Buttonbush *Cephalanthus occidentalis*	Gray Dogwood *Cornus racemosa*	Silky Dogwood or Swamp Dogwood *Cornus obliqua*	Eastern Witch Hazel *Hamamelis virginiana*	Elderberry *Sambucus canadensis*	False Indigo *Amorpha fruticosa*	Golden Currant *Ribes odoratum*
8-12 ft. tall 8+ ft. wide	8 ft. tall 12+ ft. wide	8 ft. tall 12+ ft. wide	10 ft. tall 10 ft. wide	10 ft. tall 8 ft. wide	8 ft. tall 6 ft. wide	5 ft. tall 5 ft. wide
June-August	May-July	May-July	October-November	June-July	May-June	April-June
white	small, white	small, white	yellow	white	purple and gold	yellow
flowers	flowers, fall color	bark, flowers	flowers	flowers	flowers	
general cover, clumps or thickets; butterfly/moth nectar, insect food, nutlets	general cover, clumps or thickets; butterfly/moth larval food, insect food, fall fruit for migrating birds	general cover, clumps or thickets; butterfly/moth larval food, insect food, summer fruit	general cover; insect food, seeds	general cover; insect food, summer fruit	general cover; butterfly/moth nectar, butterfly/moth larval food, insect food, seeds	general cover; butterfly/moth nectar, hummingbird nectar, summer fruit
moist, wet, tolerates clay soils	dry, moist	moist, wet	moist	moist, wet	moist, wet, tolerates clay soils	dry, moist
Fragrant balls of white flowers one of the best nectar sources for butterflies, insects and hummingbirds; nutlets eaten by wood ducks and birds; locate in depression where water pools after rain; mulch and water during dry summers; forms thickets along shorelines	Songbirds, quail and grouse eat white to gray berries; flower clusters furnish nectar and pollen for insects; larval food for moths; forms multi-stemmed thickets; upper branches excellent nest sites for songbirds	Wood ducks, quail, turkey and mammals feed on berries; flower clusters furnish nectar and pollen for insects; larval food for moths; attractive red bark in winter; forms multi-stemmed thickets; stabilizes streambanks	One of the last Midwest shrubs to bloom; sweetly-scented flowers pollinated by the last autumn insects (flies, bees); leaves, shoots and bark browsed by deer and rabbits; seeds eaten by turkey and grouse; adapted to north- and east-facing slopes, streambanks	Large flower clusters nectar and pollen for insects; fruits eaten by mammals (raccoons, squirrels), songbirds and quail	Nectar source for butterflies and bees; seeds eaten by quail and other birds; butterfly larval source (silver-spotted skipper—largest Midwest skipper, dogface sulphur, wild indigo dusky wing); red-wing blackbirds nest in branches	Small clusters of fragrant, tubular flowers nectar for hummingbirds and butterflies; berries eaten by birds and mammals; lacks spines

Small & Medium Shrubs
Adapted to Full Sun (continued)

NAME	Leadplant *Amorpha canescens*	Missouri Gooseberry *Ribes missouriense*	New Jersey Tea *Ceanothus americanus*	Ninebark *Physocarpus opulifolius*	Pasture Rose *Rosa carolina*	Prairie Willow *Salix humilis*
SIZE	3 ft. tall 3 ft. wide	3 ft. tall 6 ft. wide	3 ft. tall 3 ft. wide	8 ft. tall 8 ft. wide	2-3 ft. tall 4+ ft. wide	6 ft. tall 6+ ft. wide
WHEN DOES IT FLOWER?	May-August	April-May	May-June	May-June	May-June	March-May
FLOWER COLOR	blue, purple	yellowish-white	small, white	white	pink	small, yellow
UNIQUE OR ATTRACTIVE FEATURES	flowers, leaves		flowers, leaves	bark, flowers	flowers, fall color	flowers
WHAT WILDLIFE COVER & FOOD DOES IT PROVIDE?	butterfly/moth nectar, insect food, seeds	general cover; butterfly/moth nectar, hummingbird nectar, summer fruit	butterfly/moth nectar, butterfly/moth larval food, insect food, hummingbird nectar, summer fruit	general cover; butterfly/moth nectar, insect food, seeds	general cover, clumps or thickets; insect food, winter fruit	general cover, clumps or thickets; butterfly/moth larval food, insect food, seeds
GROWS IN WHAT KIND OF SOIL?	dry, tolerates clay soils	dry, moist	dry, tolerates clay soils	dry, moist	dry	dry, moist
COMMENTS	Dense purple flower spikes nectar for butterflies and bees; mammals graze on stems, grayish leaves; may die back during winter; drought tolerant	Small clusters of white flowers furnish nectar for hummingbirds and butterflies; larval food for gray comma butterfly; berries eaten by birds and mammals; thorny clumps provide cover	Fragrant white flowers furnish nectar to butterflies, bees and hummingbirds; seeds eaten by birds; larval food for mottled dusky wing butterfly; tea made from leaves	Flower clusters furnish nectar and pollen to butterflies, bees, beetles and other insects; dry clusters of papery fruits split to expose seeds, eaten by birds; unique bark peels off in many strips	Flowers provide pollen for insects, especially bumblebees; rose hips (high in vitamin C) eaten by birds; a shorter native rose; short prickles; spreads by underground stems	Leaves emerge early, offers important early larval food for butterflies (mourning cloak, viceroy, red-spotted purple) and moths (cecropia, scalloped owlet, sphinxes, underwings); insect and wind pollinated; male and female flowers on separate bushes; transplants well or start from seeds; unlike most willows, difficult to grow from stem cuttings; prefers drier soil; fire prevents spread on prairies; avoid planting near underground pipes or foundations

		SUMACS		
Southern Arrowwood *Viburnum dentatum*	Spicebush *Lindera benzoin*	Fragrant Sumac *Rhus aromatica*	Flameleaf Sumac or Winged Sumac *Rhus copallina*	Smooth Sumac *Rhus glabra*
8 ft. tall 10+ ft. wide	7 ft. tall 7 ft. wide	3-5 ft. tall 5-12 ft. wide	8 ft. tall 8+ ft. wide	10 ft. tall 6+ ft. wide
May-June	March-May	March-April	May-July	May-July
small, white	yellow	yellow	white	white
flowers	flowers, leaves, fall color	flowers, leaves, fall color	leaves, fall color	fall color
general cover, clumps or thickets; winter fruit, butterfly/moth nectar, butterfly/moth larval food, insect food, seeds	general cover; butterfly/moth larval food, insect food, fall fruit for migrating birds	general cover, clumps or thickets; butterfly/moth larval food, insect food, summer fruit, seeds	general cover, clumps or thickets; butterfly/moth nectar, butterfly/moth larval food, insect food, seeds	clumps or thickets; butterfly/moth nectar, butterfly/moth larval food, insect food, seeds
moist	moist, wet	dry, moist	dry, moist, grows well in acidic, nutrient-poor soils	dry, moist, tolerates clay soils
Fruits eaten by birds and mammals; flower clusters furnish butterfly and insect nectar; larval food for moths (hummingbird clearwing, rosy hook-tip); transplants well; spreads by root suckers; good border plant	Glossy, bright-red fruits eaten by birds and mammals; primary larval food for spicebush swallowtail butterfly; fragrant flowers furnish early nectar and pollen for insects; leaves once used as spice, aromatic when crushed, turn bright yellow in fall	Hairy, red berries eaten by birds and mammals; flowers with early pollen for insects; larval food for red-banded hairstreak butterfly and regal moth; spreads by root suckers; leaves are aromatic when crushed; three-leaf pattern similar to poison ivy but distinguished by no stalk on middle leaflet; spreads by underground stems	Compact cluster of seeds eaten by birds and mammals; good summer nectar and pollen source for insects; larval food for red-banded butterfly and regal moth; scarlet red fall color; leaves winged; spreads by underground stems	Compact cluster of seeds eaten by birds; larval food for regal moth; orange-red fall color; spreads by underground stems

Mark Sullivan

Shrubs and Small Trees Furnish Cover for Nesting

Clumps or groupings of native shrubs offer not only a smorgasbord of flowers and fruits for wildlife to eat, they provide cover in which to escape from predators and build nests. Wildlife can be attracted to individual plants but are much more likely to visit your property if several individuals of each species are planted together.

Compact, multi-stemmed native shrubs, such as hawthorns, hollies and viburnums, furnish premium nesting sites for songbirds, insects and other smaller wildlife. The thorns of hawthorns, native roses and wild blackberries offer protection from many predators. The dense growth helps conceal a nest from predators, and the tangle of thorns and small branches makes the nest hard to reach for larger animals such as raccoons. Scattered rows of shrubs can also serve as transition plantings between shade and sun landscapes. Straight rows appear contrived and unnatural.

ABOVE *The nectar inside flowers that grow on vines, such as the trumpet creeper on the next page, are an important food source for the delicate, but territorial, ruby-throated hummingbird. Chapter Six contains a chart of plants especially attractive to hummingbirds.*

Vines

One last group of sun-loving plants to consider in your landscape is native vines. Because of the way they grow, perennial vines require periodic pruning and should not be grown against wooden houses or other painted surfaces. Although some vines tolerate partial shade, growing vines in full sun increases flower and fruit production. To guide the growth of vines, provide structural support with trellises, wire, fences, driftwood or rocks. Vines near bird feeders furnish songbirds with great escape cover from predators such as sharp-shinned hawks.

Hummingbirds are especially attracted to the tube-like flowers of the orange trumpet creeper (*Campsis radicans*) and the native yellow honeysuckle (*Lonicera flava*). Many birds and mammals feed on the fruits of other perennial native vines such as the American bittersweet (*Celastrus scandens*), various species of grapes (*Vitis spp.*) and Virginia creeper (*Parthenocissus quinquefolia*).

Jim Rathert

bird and *butterfly landscapes*

Jim Rathert

Chapter Six

*W*ith a large yard or several acres of land, you can plant a wide array of native trees, shrubs, wildflowers and grasses to provide habitat for many types of local or resident and migrant wildlife. If you have a small yard, consider targeting your landscaping efforts to one or two specific wildlife groups. The two most popular groups of wildlife that people enjoy around their homes are birds and butterflies. Even if your yard is large, you can landscape parts of it for various types of birds or butterflies. Keep this in mind for areas close to your house where you can observe wildlife throughout the year.

Of the three wildlife habitat components—food, water and cover—the search for food is probably the single, most compelling reason for birds and butterflies to visit your property. Focus on furnishing food, then supplement your efforts with water and cover as space allows. Because plant selection becomes even more crucial with space limitations, the native landscape food plants for various wildlife groups listed here are very focused.

Native landscaping to provide food for birds and butterflies in the central Midwest is broken down into these categories:

Nectar for adult butterflies and food sources for
  butterfly caterpillars
Nectar for hummingbirds
Summer fruits for summer resident birds and mammals
Fall fruits for migrating songbirds
Winter fruits for winter resident birds and mammals

Native Landscaping for Butterflies

Most adult butterflies worship the sun. The sun warms their bodies and increases their metabolic rate high enough for flight. Butterflies actively fly around on warm, sunny days but become inactive on cool, cloudy days. In the mornings, butterflies often bask with their wings open and lie perpendicular to the sun for maximum solar heat. Be sure to keep flat rocks around your butterfly nectar plants, positioned to collect heat from the morning sun for basking sites early in the day.

After warming up, butterflies—with their straw-like mouthparts—seek out nectar-producing plants for a high-calorie drink. Hungry adult butterflies may sip nectar from the flowers of many different native plants. Butterflies are especially lured to plants that produce clusters of small flowers, such as milkweeds, or plants with broad petals, such as coneflowers. The petals serve as landing pads where they can sit and drink. Most large butterflies do not perch on flowers that hang down or droop.

Butterflies generally favor white, blue, pink and purple flowers. The length of a species' mouthpart seems to influence these preferences. Long tubular flowers, such

Jim Rathert

CHAPTER COVER PAGE *In the late fall and winter, watch for flocks of cedar waxwings feeding on winter fruits or roosting in trees.*
ABOVE *Butterfly gardens are among the most popular native landscapes and can be successful even when small. Baltimore checkerspots are found throughout the Midwest. Adults frequent flowers, animal droppings, mud puddles and other moist spots.*

Jim Rathert

as the beard-tongues, are visited only by swallowtails and other butterflies with long mouthparts. One exception to color preference is the coral hairstreak butterfly, which prefers nectar from the orange butterflyweed.

When you plan your butterfly landscape, strive for blooming each month from early spring to late fall. If you discover gaps in your flowering chronology, consider trimming back some buds to delay blooming. Butterflies are usually attracted to the dominant flowering plants. For this reason, it is better to clump your nectar sources in patches rather than scatter single, isolated plants throughout the yard. For easier butterfly watching and close-up photography, avoid locating the nectar plants in windy areas.

Don't Forget the Caterpillars

Getting a close look at butterflies on the wing is sometimes challenging—not so with caterpillars. If you grow the right caterpillar food or host plants for the butterflies you see flying around in your neighborhood, you stand a good chance of seeing caterpillars up close.

Most adults sip nectar from a variety of flowers, but the vast majority of butterflies lay their eggs on or near specific host plants that contain certain nutrients the caterpillars need for proper growth. In fact, the common names of several butterflies originate from their host plants, such as the spicebush swallowtail and the hackberry butterfly. This adaptation is apparently so strong that most caterpillars starve to death if they cannot find their specific host plants soon after emerging from their egg cases.

Jim Rathert

Lepidoptera—butterflies and moths—are probably the most loved and celebrated of all the insects. In almost all the world's cultures, they have inspired centuries of poetry, song, dance and visual arts.

Some butterfly caterpillars even gain a chemical protection from their host plants which continues into adulthood. For example, monarch butterfly caterpillars feed exclusively on milkweeds. Chemicals in the milky latex of this plant make both the caterpillar and adult unpalatable to insect–eating birds.

If you watch caterpillars up close, you can see they are undulating, accordion-like, eating machines. Caterpillars are the main feeding and growing stage in the butterfly life cycle. As they eat, caterpillars grow dramatically, doubling and re-doubling their size every few days. As they get large, caterpillars eat substantial amounts of their host plants. Plants dotted with partially eaten leaves can become ugly, so you may want to locate caterpillar host plants away from high-visibility areas of your property.

The best native Midwest nectar plants for adult butterflies and host plants for caterpillars are listed here. These plants are grouped into native wildflowers, water plants, shrubs and trees that large, adult butterflies visit regularly for nectar. The majority of these plants are perennials, adapted to full sun environments for maximum nectar production. For the sun to reach most of your plants, arrange wildflowers in tiers or a stair-step design.

LEFT *Caterpillars turn into moths and butterflies, and with their fuzz and bright colors, a closer look is hard to resist. Caterpillars eat plants but seldom cause any serious damage to native plant species. Charts of butterfly nectar and caterpillar host plants appear on the next page.*

Best Butterfly Nectar Plants

The best native Midwest nectar plants for adult butterflies and some that are host plants for caterpillars are listed here. These plants are grouped into the native wildflowers, water plants, and shrubs and trees that large, adult butterflies visit regularly for nectar. The majority of these plants are perennials and adapted to full sun environments for maximum nectar production.

WILDFLOWERS

NAME	Black-eyed Susan *Rudbeckia hirta*	Butterflyweed *Asclepias tuberosa*	Culver's Root *Veronicastrum virginicum*	Eastern Blazing Star *Liatris scariosa*
SIZE	18-36"	18-36"	36-54"	30-48"
WHEN DOES IT BLOOM?	June-July	June-August	June-September	August-September
COMMENTS	Good nectar food source for many butterflies and other insects	Excellent nectar food source for a variety of butterflies, especially the monarch and coral and coral hairstreak butterflies; larval food source for monarch caterpillars; slow-growing plant with attractive, showy flowers	Candelabra-shaped flower spikes are excellent nectar food sources for many butterflies and other insects	Perhaps the best blazing star nectar food source for butterflies, hummingbirds and other insects
FOR FLOWER COLOR, SOIL TYPE, ETC., SEE:	page 88	page 91	page 90	page 88

NAME	Ohio Horsemint or Pagoda Plant *Blephilla ciliata*	Pale Purple Coneflower *Echinacea pallida*	Prairie Blazing Star *Liatris pycnostachya*	Purple Coneflower *Echinacea purpurea*
SIZE	18-24"	24-36"	30-54"	28-48"
WHEN DOES IT BLOOM?	May-August	June-July	July-September	July-August
COMMENTS	Excellent nectar food source for a variety of butterflies and other insects; attractive flower arrangement of round clusters stacked on top of each resembles a pagoda roof.	Excellent nectar food sources for butterflies and other insects; look for crab spiders ambushing insects on flower heads; white pollen distinguishes it from the glade coneflower	One of the best nectar food sources for butterflies (especially swallowtails), hummingbirds and other insects	Good nectar food source for butterflies and other insects
FOR FLOWER COLOR, SOIL TYPE, ETC., SEE:	page 91	page 89	page 89	page 90

Garden Phlox	Glade Coneflower	Indian Paintbrush	Lanceleaf Coreopsis	New England Aster
Phlox paniculata	*Echinacea simulata*	*Castilleja coccinea*	*Coreopsis lanceolata*	*Aster novae-angliae*
36-54"	24-36"	8-18"	12-24"	48-72"
July-September	June-July	April-June	May-June	August-October
Tall, late-blooming perennial with pyramidal flower clusters; furnishes good nectar food source for hummingbirds, butterflies, and other insects	One of the best nectar food sources for butterflies and other insects; look for crab spiders ambushing insects on flower heads; yellow pollen distinguishes it from the pale purple coneflower	Color varies from red to orange to yellow; red and orange flowers are magnets for butterflies and hummingbirds	This species and its cousin, the large-flowered coreopsis (*Coreopsis grandiflora*) which blooms about a month later, are excellent nectar food sources for butterflies and many small bees; with its small leaves and large flower heads, lanceleaf coreopsis is well adapted to dry, rocky, glade habitats	Largest aster in Midwest; although color variable, dark purple common; excellent late nectar food source for migrating monarchs and other autumn insects; host plant for pearl crescent butterfly larvae
page 90	page 89	page 91	page 91	page 88

Purple Prairie Clover	Rattlesnake Master	Rose verbena	Shining Blue Star	Western Wallflower
Dalea purpurea	*Eryngium yuccifolium*	*Glandularia canadensis*	*Amsonia illustris*	*Erysimum capitatum*
18-24"	36-54"	6-12"	24-36"	12-36"
June-August	July-August	March-October	April-May	May-July
This species and its cousin, white prairie clover (*Dalea candida*), produce densely-packed flowers on cylindrical flower heads that bloom from the bottom up; larval food source for dogface sulphur butterfly; native bees run around the head in circles collecting the pollen—fun to observe	Numerous round, white flowers, thick stems and basal leaves that resemble yuccas; excellent nectar food source for butterflies, bumblebees and other insects	Good early nectar food source for many butterflies and insects	Numerous star-shaped flowers are excellent nectar food sources for butterflies; larval food source for snowberry clearsing moth	Showy, biennial is excellent nectar food source for butterflies and other insects; reproduces by seeds, but not reliable to return each year
page 92	page 92	page 93	page 93	page 93

Best Butterfly Nectar Plants (continued)

WILDFLOWERS *continued*   WATER PLANTS

NAME	Wild Bergamot *Monarda fistulosa*	Yellow Coneflower *Echinacea paradoxa*	Cardinal Flower *Lobelia cardinalis*	Marsh or Swamp Milkweed *Asclepias incarmata*
SIZE	30-48"	24-42"	24-48"	40-60"
WHEN DOES IT BLOOM?	May-August	May-June	August-September	June-August
COMMENTS	Flowers with arching lower lips form round clusters at top of square stems; good nectar food source for many native bees, butterflies and hummingbirds	Good nectar food source for butterflies and other insects	One of the best nectar sources for the beautiful cloudless sulphur butterfly, as well as hummingbirds	Excellent nectar food source for butterflies, especially monarchs; larval food source for monarch caterpillars
FOR FLOWER COLOR, SOIL TYPE, ETC., SEE:		page 90	page 89	page 90

SHRUBS AND TREES *continued*

NAME	Eastern Redbud *Cercis canadensis*	Fragrant Sumac *Rhus aromatica*	Spicebush *Lindera benzoin*	Wild Plum *Prunus americana*
SIZE	15-20'	3-5'	6-8'	15-18'
WHEN DOES IT BLOOM?	March-April	March-April	March-May	March-April
COMMENTS	Flower clusters arise directly from branches and trunk; serve as excellent, early nectar and pollen source for many insects	Flowers furnish early pollen source for many insects; larval food source for red-banded hairstreak butterfly and regal moth	Fragrant flowers furnish early nectar and pollen source for many early butterflies and insects; primary larval food source for spicebush swallowtail butterfly	Excellent early nectar source for early butterflies such as the spring azure (first native butterfly species to emerge from overwintering pupae); flowers also furnish early pollen food source for many insects; larval food sources for many butterflies, such as hairstreaks and viceroys, and moths, such as cecropia and sphinxs
FOR FLOWER COLOR, SOIL TYPE, ETC., SEE:	page 102	page 109	page 109	page 105

SHRUBS AND TREES

Pickerel Weed *Pontederia cordata*	Water Willow *Justicia americana*	Blackberries, Dewberries and Raspberries *Rubus spp.*	Buttonbush *Cephalanthus occidentalis*
12-40"	10-20"	3-6'	8-12'
June-October	June-October	April-June	June-August
Attractive flower spike and arrow-shaped leaves; roots in water with stems emerging; good nectar source for variety of butterflies and other insects	Small, orchid-like flower is excellent nectar food source for a variety of insects, especially skipper and swallowtail butterflies	Excellent nectar and pollen food source for many insects; high-sugar, fleshy fruits eaten by resident birds and mammals	The best shrub nectar source for butterflies and many other insects and hummingbirds; fragrant, balls of white flowers form a star burst pattern
page 92	page 93	page 106	page 107

Best Butterfly Caterpillar Host Plants

Select these food or host plants to attract caterpillars of some of the most showy and common butterflies in the central Midwest. The majority of these plants are perennials that grow best in full sun. Butterflies are listed alphabetically by common name, followed by the specific native host plant(s) preferred. There are excellent field guides to butterflies and moths available, and they can help you identify and learn more about the species that visit your yard.

BUTTERFLY SPECIES	American Painted Lady	Black Swallowtail	Dogface Sulphur	Giant Swallowtail	Great Spangled Fritillary
HOST PLANT(S)	Pussy Toes *(Antennaria parlinii)*	Golden Alexander *(Zizia aurea)*	False Indigo *(Amorpha fruiticosa)* Prairie Clovers *(Dalea purpurea and Dalea candida)* Leadplant *(Amorpha canescens)*	Hoptree *(Ptelea trifoiata)* Prickly-Ash *(Zanthoxylum americanum)*	Violets *(Viola spp.)*
PLANT INFORMATION FOUND ON:	page 69	page 90	pages 107, 108	page 104	page 69

SPECIES	Question Mark Butterfly	Red Spotted Purple	Regal Fritillary	Snout Butterfly	Spicebush Swallowtail
HOST PLANT(S)	Hackberries *(Celtis spp.)*	Willows *(Salix spp.)* Wild Cherries *(Prunus spp.)* Wild Crabapples *(Malus spp.)*	Violets *(Viola spp.)*	Hackberry *(Celtis occidentalis)* Sugarberry *(Celtis laevigata)*	Spicebush *(Lindera benzoin)* Sassafras *(Sassafras albidum)*
PLANT INFORMATION FOUND ON:	page 60	pages 65, 102, 104	page 69	page 60	pages 109, 61

Hackberry Butterfly	Missouri Woodland Swallowtail	Monarch	Mourning Cloak	Olive Hairstreak	Pearl Crescent
Hackberry (*Celtis occidentalis*) Sugarberry (*Celtis laevigata*)	Golden Alexander (*Zizia aurea*)	Milkweeds (*Asclepias spp.*), such as Butterflyweed (*Asclepias tuberosa*)	Willows (*Salix spp.*) Hackberries (*Celtis spp.*) Birch (*Betula spp.*)	Eastern Red Cedar (*Juniperus virginiana*)	Asters (*Aster spp.*), especially New England Aster (*Aster novae-angliae*)
page 60	page 90	page 91	page 60	page 102	page 88

Tiger Swallowtail	Viceroy	Zebra Zwallowtail			
Eastern Hoptree (*Ptelea trifoliata*) Prickly-ash (*Zanthoxylum americanum*)	Willows (*Salix spp.*), especially Black Willow (*Salix nigra*) Wild Cherries (*Prunus spp.*)	Pawpaw (*Asimina triloba*)			
page 104	pages 60, 102	page 104			

Jim Rathert

Native Landscaping for Hummingbirds

Hummingbirds are unbelievable creatures to watch. They weigh about as much as a penny, but their hearts beat more than 10 times a second and their wings beat from 80 to 200 times a second. To accomplish these feats, they sip energy-rich nectar from flowers or sugar water from feeders. They battle each other aggressively over these foods, and males fly in sweeping, 30-foot-high J-shaped patterns to attract females.

In addition to maintaining hummingbird feeders around your house, you can plant nectar-producing wildflowers, bushes, trees and vines to draw hummingbirds to your property. Hummingbirds generally are attracted to nectar plants that produce red, orange and pink tube-shaped flowers, such as columbine, spotted touch-me-nots and purple beard-tongue. To improve your chances of getting hummingbirds to notice your plantings, cluster your plants together to offer a bigger splash of color.

The following list of hummingbird nectar plants highlights the best native Midwest nectar food plants for hummingbirds. These plants are categorized into native wildflowers, water plants and shrubs and trees. The plants are perennials that grow and bloom best in full sun, unless otherwise noted. To maximize flower production, arrange your hummingbird nectar plants in tiers or a stair-step design. To enjoy hummingbirds all during the warm months, plan to have a couple of these plants blooming each month.

ABOVE *Ruby-throated hummingbirds rarely sit still. This one is poised at the edge of a sugar water feeder. See page 161-162 for tips about placing and taking care of feeders.*

Best Hummingbird Nectar Plants

Many native plants, such as those listed here, will help attract hummingbirds. Some are considered to be good sources for nectar; others are excellent. Keep in mind that native vines, such as trumpet creeper (*Campsis radicans*), yellow honeysuckle (*Lonicera flava*) and crossvine (*Bignonia capreolata*), are also attractive to hummingbirds.

WILDFLOWERS

NAME	Bluebells *Mertensia virginica*	Columbine *Aquilegia canadensis*	Eastern Blazing Star *Liatris scariosa*	Fire Pink *Silene virginica*
SIZE	18-24"	20-30"	30-48"	8-20"
WHEN DOES IT BLOOM?	April-May	April-June	August-September	April-June
SOURCE FOR NECTAR?	good	excellent	good	excellent
COMMENTS	Inch-long, nodding, trumpet-like flowers furnish good nectar food source for hummingbirds	Hummingbirds relish long-blooming flowers for nectar food source; leaf miner insects feed on leaves and produce winding, light trails	Good nectar food source for hummingbirds	Excellent early-flowering nectar food source for hummingbirds
FOR FLOWER COLOR, SOIL TYPE, ETC., SEE:	page 68	page 68	page 88	page 90
NAME	Garden Phlox *Phlox paniculata*	Horsemint or Bee Balm *Monarda bradburiana*	Indian Paintbrush *Castilleja coccinea*	Pale Jewelweed *Impatiens pallida*
SIZE	36-54"	12-24"	8-18"	36-60"
WHEN DOES IT BLOOM?	July-September	April-June	April-June	May-October
SOURCE FOR NECTAR?	good	good	excellent	good
COMMENTS	This tall, late-blooming perennial with its pyramidal flower clusters furnishes a good nectar food source for hummingbirds, butterflies, and other insects	Good nectar food source for native bees, butterflies and hummingbirds	Color varies from red to orange to yellow; red and orange flowers are magnets for hummingbirds; color comes from flower bracts	Cornucopia-shaped flower is a hummingbird nectar magnet
FOR FLOWER COLOR, SOIL TYPE, ETC., SEE:	page 90	page 68	page 91	page 69

Best Hummingbird
Nectar Plants (continued)

NAME	Prairie Blazing Star *Liatris pycnostachya*	Purple Beardtongue *Penstemon cobaea var. purpureus*	Royal Catchfly *Silene regia*	Spotted Jewelweed *Impatiens capensis*
SIZE	30-54"	18-30"	24-48"	36-60"
WHEN DOES IT BLOOM?	July-September	May-June	June-September	May-October
SOURCE FOR NECTAR?	good	excellent	excellent	excellent
COMMENTS	Good nectar food sources for hummingbirds; tall flower spike blooms for long period	Large, tubular flowers are spectacular in beauty; excellent nectar food source for hummingbirds and large bees	Bright-red, tubular flowers are excellent summer nectar food source for hummingbirds	Cornucopia-shaped flower is a hummingbird nectar magnet
FOR FLOWER COLOR, SOIL TYPE, ETC., SEE:	page 88	page 92	page 93	page 69

SHRUBS AND TREES

NAME	Buttonbush *Cephalanthus occidentalis*	Golden Currant *Ribes odoratum*	Green Hawthorn *Crataegus viridis*	Missouri Gooseberry *Ribes missouriense*
SIZE	18-12'	4-5'	20-25'	2-4'
WHEN DOES IT BLOOM?	June-August	April-June	May-June	April-May
SOURCE FOR NECTAR?	excellent	good	good	good
COMMENTS	Excellent nectar food source for hummingbirds; the fragrant, balls of white flowers form a star burst pattern	Small clusters of fragrant, golden-yellow, tubular flowers furnish nectar for hummingbirds and butterflies; berries eaten several birds and mammals	Along with other hawthorns, green haw produces good nectar source for hummingbirds; small, dense and thorny branches furnish excellent bird nesting and roosting cover	Small clusters of flowers furnish nectar for hummingbirds and butterflies; berries eaten by several birds and mammals; thorny clusters of trunks provide nesting and roosting bird cover
FOR FLOWER COLOR, SOIL TYPE, ETC., SEE:	page 107	page 107	page 103	page 108

WATER PLANTS

Wild Bergamont	Cardinal Flower	Copper Iris	Rose Mallow	Rose Turtlehead
Monarda fistulosa	*Lobelia cardinalis*	*Iris fulva*	*Hibiscus lasiocarpos*	*Chelone obliqua*
30-48"	24-48"	18-30"	42-72"	24-42"
May-August	August-September	May-June	August-September	September-October
good	excellent	good	good	good
Good nectar food source for native bees, butterflies and hummingbirds	One of the best nectar sources for hummingbirds and the beautiful cloudless sulphur butterfly	Only reddish iris in the Midwest; good nectar food source for hummingbirds	Large, shrub-like, non-woody, robust native plant has one of the largest flowers (about 6" across) in the Midwest; deep-red center of white flower acts as a nectar guide for hummingbirds	This species and its cousin, the white turtlehead (*Chelone glabra*), are excellent late-season nectar food sources for hummingbirds and bumblebees
	page 89	page 90	page 92	page 92

New Jersey Tea	Ohio Buckeye	Red Buckeye	Tuliptree	
Ceanothus americanus	*Aesculus glabra*	*Aesculus pavia*	*Liriodendron tulipifera*	
2-3'	30-35'	15-20'	70-80'	
May-June	April-May	April-May	April-May	
good	good	excellent	good	
Fragrant white flower clusters furnish nectar to butterflies, bees, and hummingbirds; seeds/nutlets eaten by several birds	Clusters of showy flowers furnish nectar for hummingbirds	Showy, tubular, red flowers are magnets for hummingbirds; flowering is timed to return of migrating hummingbirds	Hummingbirds and many insects feed on nectar and pollen of attractive, large, yellow flowers trimmed in orange	
page 108	page 61	page 104	page 61	**127**

Summer Fruits for Resident Birds and Mammals

The fruits of native plants that appear in mid- to late summer generally are high in sugar and low in fat. As fruits ripen, they typically change from green to red to blue or purple. This color change—called a fruit flag—signals to the summer resident birds and mammals that the fruits are ready to be eaten, either hanging on the plant or falling to the ground. This fruit flag is especially important to birds because most species lack a sense of smell and their sense of taste is not well developed. Mammals, on the other hand, have a well-developed sense of both smell and taste that helps them locate ripe fruits. If the fruits go uneaten for long, they break down quickly because of the high-sugar content, and the seeds do not get dispersed.

Plants with juicy fruits have strategies to get their seeds scattered to new areas where more plants could grow. Most summer fruits, such as blueberries, mulberries and blackberries, contain small seeds. Robins, bluebirds, many thrushes and other resident birds—as well as resident mammals such as raccoons, chipmunks, foxes and squirrel—eat the sweet fruits containing the small seeds. Later, the animal regurgitates or defecates some of the undigested seeds away from the parent plant, but still in the general vicinity where conditions are favorable

Jim Rathert

for new plants to grow. If the seeds fell to the ground beneath the parent plant and were not eaten by a passing animal, the young plants would then have to compete with their parent for sunlight, water and nutrients. Plants package or enclose seeds inside a fruit so animals will carry the seeds away.

The timing of fruits ripening is also important. It typically occurs after the big insect hatch of the spring and early summer. As insect numbers decline, many birds appear to shift their diets from insects to fruits. Birds and mammals obtain energy from eating the fruits while plants get their seeds dispersed. Both types of organisms have evolved an interdependency upon each other. If you would like to observe this interdependency on your property, select shrubs and trees that produce high-sugar, summer fruits. Keep plant dimensions in mind when you consider locations for these native plants.

Jim Rathert

LEFT *Blackberries provide birds, mammals and people with delicious summer fruit.* **ABOVE** *Chipmunks—with their seemingly endless energy— are great fun to watch.*

Summer Fruits for Resident Birds & Mammals

Here is a selection of native plants with summer fruits that are high in sugar and low in fat for summer residents birds and mammals.

BLUEBERRIES

NAME	Blackberries, Dewberries and Raspberries *Rubus spp.*	Black Cherry *Prunus serotina*	Deerberry or Highbush Huckleberry *Vaccinium stamineum*	Farkleberry or Highbush Blueberry *Vaccinium arboreum*
COMMENTS	Excellent high-sugar, fleshy fruits for resident birds, mammals; prickly brambles furnish cover	Songbirds, chipmunks relish fruits and disperse seeds; larval food source for many moths (cecropia, blind-eyed sphinx, wild cherry sphinx, skiff) and some butterflies (tiger swallowtail, red-spotted purple)	Fruits eaten by mammals, summer resident birds; larval food source for Henry's elfin butterfly and yellow-washed metarranthis moth	Fruits larger than deerberry and lowbush blueberries, not as palatable due to mealy texture; eaten by some mammals, summer resident birds; larval food source for Henry's elfin butterfly and yellow-washed metarranthis moth
FOR FLOWER COLOR, SOIL TYPE, ETC., SEE:	page 106	page 60	page 106	page 106

NAME	Elderberry *Sambucus canadensis*	Fragrant Sumac *Rhus aromatica*	Golden Currant *Ribes odoratum*	Missouri Gooseberry *Ribes missouriense*
COMMENTS	Large fruits eaten by mammals (raccoons, squirrels), songbirds and quail	Hairy, red berries eaten by many birds, mammals	Fruits are eaten by birds, mammals; forms small clusters of very fragrant, golden-yellow tubular flowers that produce nectar eaten by hummingbirds and butterflies	Berries eaten by birds, mammals; thorny clusters of trunks provide cover
FOR FLOWER COLOR, SOIL TYPE, ETC., SEE:	page 107	page 109	page 107	page 108

Lowbush Blueberry *Vaccinium pallidum*	Chokecherry *Prunus virginiana*	Rough-leaf Dogwood *Cornus drummondii*	Silky Dogwood or Swamp Dogwood *Cornus obliqua*	Downy Serviceberry *Amelanchier arborea*
Fruits ripen throughout a longer period than deerberry or farkleberry and are eaten by mammals, summer resident birds; larval food source for Henry's elfin butterfly and yellow-washed metarranthis moth	Songbirds, chipmunks relish fruits and disperse seeds; larval food source for tiger swallowtail butterfly and several sphinx moths, including blind-eyed and wild cherry sphinxs	Variety of songbirds, woodpeckers, mammals feed on white berries; good songbird nesting cover	Wood ducks, quail, turkey, several mammals feed on berries; attractive red bark in winter	Many birds, several mammals feed on berries; one of the first trees to flower in spring; bark has shallow, vertical grooves and rounded ridges
page 106	page 102	page 102	page 107	page 102

Pasture Rose *Rosa carolina*	Pawpaw *Asimina triloba*	Prairie Crabapple *Malus ioensis*	Red Mulberry *Morus rubra*	Wild Plum *Prunus americana*
Rose hips (fruits high in vitamin C) eaten by birds; flowers especially attractive to bummblebees	Ripe fruit tastes like banana, looks like a stubby banana; relished by raccoons, opossums	Many mammals and several ground-feeding birds eat apples	Birds, mammals relish the fleshy berries (resemble skinny black-berry); fruits ripen at different times over several-week period	Some larger birds feed on fruit; mainly eaten by mammals (fox, raccoons)
page 108	page 104	page 104	page 61	page 105

Fall Fruits for Migrating Songbirds

Only a few native plants produce fruits high in fat and low in sugar that ripen in late summer and early fall. High-fat fruits are especially important to migrating birds because fats contain about twice the energy per unit of weight as sugars. Mammals, including humans, prefer sweet-tasting fruits and not the high-fat fruits which tend to taste sour. For migrating birds such as waxwings, catbirds, orioles, tanagers and thrushes that may travel long distances, energy is more important than taste.

Unlike resident birds, migrating birds are not familiar with the habitat and can't afford to spend much time and energy looking around for high-fat fruits. Besides fruit flags, many native plants have adapted to using another kind of signal for seed dispersal by migrating birds. Spicebush shrubs, Virginia creeper vines, flowering dogwood trees and others all begin changing to their autumn colors of brilliant yellow, red and purple early in the fall. They are referred to as signaling plants.

Jim Rathert

When most other plants are still green, this early color change of the leaves or foliage—called foliar flags—is a vivid signal to migrating birds, besides spicing up the fall landscape for humans. These plants put much of their energy into high-fat fruit production and, without foliar flags, many of their seeds would not be dispersed. If you enjoy watching flocks of migrating birds stop and feed on your property, plant these native trees and shrubs with high-fat fall fruits.

ABOVE *Native plants produce fruits and nuts in spring, summer, fall and some persist into the winter months. As you plan, remember to choose native plants that will provide food for wildlife during more than one season. This flowering dogwood produces fruit mid-fall.*

Fall Fruits for Migrating Birds

A guide to selecting native plants that produce early fall fruits containing a high-fat and low-sugar content to benefit fall bird migrants.

		DOGWOODS	
NAME	Blackgum *Nyssa sylvatica*	Flowering Dogwood *Cornus florida*	Gray Dogwood *Cornus racemosa*
COMMENTS	Migrating songbirds relish fruits, disperse seeds	Important high-fat, red fruits for migrating songbirds, quail, turkey and several mammals	Songbirds, quail and grouse relish white to gray berries; upper branches excellent nest sites for songbirds
FOR FLOWER COLOR, SOIL TYPE, ETC., SEE:	page 60	page 102	page 107

NAME	Sassafras *Sassafras albidum*	Spicebush *Lindera benzoin*
COMMENTS	Squirrels, many migrating birds eat fruit	Glossy, bright-red fruits eaten by migrating birds, mammals
FOR FLOWER COLOR, SOIL TYPE, ETC., SEE:	page 61	page 109

Jim Rathert

Winter Fruits for Birds and Mammals

Most of the Midwest's native shrubs and trees that produce fruit in mid- to late fall have both low-fat and low-sugar fruits to resist rot. Fruits from these plants persist well into the cold weather and are eaten by birds and mammals when nothing else is available in late winter or early spring. Enriching fruits with high amounts of sugars or fats is somewhat risky for the fruiting plants and only a few have developed this strategy. The more conservative approach for most of the fruiting plants in the Midwest is to produce low-sugar and low-fat fruits, then divert some of their energy into growth and maintenance.

Native species of hollies, hawthorns, hackberries, roses and most viburnums are the conservative shrubs and trees. Also included are sumacs; their fruits contain a fair amount of fat but little flesh and persist well into the winter. Frost or fox grape vines and Eastern red cedar trees also produce low-fat, low-sugar fall fruits. Fruit-eating migrant birds on their return trip north in late winter and early spring eat these fruits, especially if there is a late-spring cold snap and few other foods are available.

ABOVE *Cedar trees, with their blue fleshy fruits, attract many birds in the winter. This American robin will not only eat the cedar tree fruit, but it will likely seek cover in the tree's thick branches at night.*

Winter Fruits for Birds & Mammals

These native plants have mid- to late-fall fruits that persist into the winter and contain a low-fat and low-sugar content. They benefit bird and mammal winter residents and early spring bird migrants.

				HAWTHORNS		HOLLIES
NAME	Beautyberry *Callicarpa americana*	Eastern Red Cedar *Juniperus virginiana*	Hackberry *Celtis occidentalis*	Cockspur Hawthorn *Crataegus crus-galli* downy hawthorn *Crataegus mollis*	Green Hawthorn *Crataegus viridis;* Washington Hawthorn *Crataegus phaenopyrum*	American Holly *Ilex opaca*
COMMENTS	Rosy-violet fruits furnish winter food for bluebirds and other species	Dense, small branches make the best winter roost for birds in the Midwest, especially at night; doves and other birds build nests in the branches; fleshy cone resembles blue berry, important winter food for mammals, birds, such as cedar waxwings returning early in the spring.	Songbirds relish fruits, dispense seeds		Birds, mammals eat the red fruits that persist into winter; dense, thorny branches are used by birds for nesting and roosting.	Songbirds eat red berries after first hard frost; evergreen, prickly leaves provide winter cover for songbirds, spring nest sites
FOR FLOWER COLOR, SOIL TYPE, ETC., SEE:	page 106	page 102	page 60	page 103	page 103	page 103

	HOLLIES *continued*				VIBURNUMS
NAME	Deciduous Holly *Ilex decidua*	Winterberry *Ilex verticillata*	Pasture Rose *Rosa carolina*	Persimmon *Diospyros virginiana*	Blackhaw *Viburnum prunifolium;* Nannyberry *Viburnum lentago* Rusty Blackhaw *Viburnum rufidulum* Southern Arrowwood *Viburnum dentatum*
COMMENTS	Songbirds, quail, opossums and other mammals eat orange-red berries in winter	Songbirds, quail, grouse, small mammals eat red-yellow berries through winter	Rose hips (fruits high in vitamin C) eaten by birds	Opossums and other mammals and fruit-eating birds relish fleshy, orange fruits, disperse seeds	Fruits eaten by birds, mammals
FOR FLOWER COLOR, SOIL TYPE, ETC., SEE:	page 103	page 104	page 108	page 61	page 105

Jim Rathert

pools, marshes *and* glades

Chapter Seven

In addition to shade and sun landscapes, there are other intriguing natural communities in the Midwest and some interesting wildlife species are drawn to these communities. You may want to duplicate one of these inviting places as a component of your landscaping plan.

Stream, pool, marsh and glade communities can all be sized down and possibly tucked into a corner of your landscape. Starting or enhancing the character of a small portion of your yard and landscaping to create one of these Midwest communities can generate an interesting focal point on your property. Do a little research, read and learn about each community. Understanding the plants, animals and their interrelationships brings a deeper appreciation for the larger versions of glades, pools and marshlands found throughout the Midwest.

Wildlife Pools Come in Many Sizes

Jim Rathert

The simplest water feature for wildlife is the birdbath. More wild animals use it if the dish portion is balanced on a low-standing clay pot and supported with rocks, although it will accumulate debris faster near the ground than if it stands on a taller pedestal. Galvanized wash tubs, pre-formed plastic pool liners and wooden barrels cut in half can also be buried in the ground to serve as simple wildlife pools. Or you can customize the shape of your water feature by using sheets of plastic liner or cement to make pools. In addition to access, perches are important for animals, especially when the water level fluctuates with evaporation. Rocks of varying sizes or pieces of cedar with a few small, protruding branches can furnish perches at different heights for birds and dragonflies or basking sites for frogs and turtles.

The most effective way to draw wildlife with water is to make it flow, drip or spray. The sound of moving water is irresistible to animals such as songbirds, frogs and small mammals. For a quick and easy source of dripping water, let an outside faucet drip into a pan, or hang a water bucket with a small hole in the bottom of it over a pan or pool. Installing a recycling pump keeps the water moving through a pool. By pumping the water uphill, you can design a series of small waterfalls for

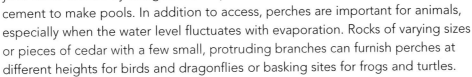

CHAPTER COVER PAGE *Green frogs tend to be solitary animals, often just one adult to a pond or pool. They eat a variety of insects and males emit a loud "bong," sometimes described as similar to the sound of a loose banjo string.* **ABOVE** *Amphibians are just a few of the animals attracted to water gardens or pools of all sizes. Birds and mammals will seek them out, too.*

139

M. Naumann

flowing water. To keep the water clear in larger water pools or water features, you can include a filtration system and use various treatments to minimize unwanted algae growth.

As you design your water feature with the characteristics of a natural pool, be sure to include submerged shelves for potted water plants to stand on. Although there are only a handful of water plants that produce nectar for butterflies and hummingbirds, water plants are very attractive and add another dimension to your property. Consider planting some emergent native water plants, or plants with roots in the water and stems and leaves above. The three-foot-tall pickerel weed has showy purple flowers to attract butterflies. Hummingbirds feed from the copper iris. Although irises grow better in saturated soil, they can grow two to three feet tall in a pot placed in shallow water. Water primrose is a good nectar source for small butterflies such as skippers. Lists of water plants that attract hummingbirds and butterflies are found in Chapter Six on pages 118-123.

Marshes

If you have a low spot or dip on your property where water stands after a rain, you may want to take advantage of this water-saturated soil and create a small marsh. To create a marsh, dig out a small hole, fill it with a rich soil (high in organic matter) and keep it saturated with water from a garden hose. Soil

ABOVE *Pickerel weed is an especially attractive water plant.* **RIGHT, TOP** *This skipper has found a spot on a water willow, which is adapted to gravelly soil and is fairly easy to grow.* **RIGHT, BOTTOM** *Dragonflies are gaining popularity among wildlife watchers.*

Dave Tylka

with a high clay content tends to hold water well. If the soil where you would like to locate a mini-marsh tends to absorb the water, line the depression with a piece or two of six-millimeter plastic before you refill the hole with rich soil.

For an even smaller space, fill up a wooden half-barrel, galvanized tub or plastic liner with organically rich soil to mimic a marsh community. To help collect and retain water, dig a hole and sink your container in the ground. Slope the surrounding soil so rain will drain into it. Make sure it can be reached with a hose in case it doesn't rain for awhile. For any of these small-scale marshes, you may want to keep your plants in pots because most water plants can spread rapidly with underground stems or rhizomes. Marsh plants generally do best if planted in rich black mud. Supplement them with well-decomposed compost or other weed-free organic matter if the soil is poor.

Some marsh plants grow large. The woody shrub buttonbush and a shrub-like, large plant called rose mallow both thrive in water-saturated soils or in shallow water. Buttonbush is one of the best butterfly nectar sources in the Midwest and, under ideal conditions, grows more than 10 feet tall. The round, white flower clusters take on a beautiful star-burst pattern. Rose mallow grows up to six feet tall and has large, white flowers with red centers that attract humming-birds. If you have room on your property, both of these species not only produce beautiful flowers, but also are highly beneficial to wildlife.

In the wild, several colorful wildflowers grow in saturated soil at the water's edge and are popular with wildlife. The scarlet-red cardinal flower and its cousin, the blue lobelia, both grow one to three feet tall. Both of these lobelias attract

Jim Rathert

141

Jim Rathert

butterflies and hummingbirds to their tubular flowers. About the same size are the white turtlehead and rose turtlehead. They also attract both butterflies and hummingbirds. The copper iris and the southern blue flag both grow one to three feet tall. Their tubular flowers are too long for most butterflies to reach down inside, but they are visited by hummingbirds. In the three- to five-foot-tall class, the pink marsh milkweed, spotted touch-me-not and yellow pale touch-me-not attract both butterflies and hummingbirds. Lists on pages 118-121 and 125-127 in Chapter Six include native plants that are especially attractive to butterflies and hummingbirds.

Glade Communities

Xeriscapes are landscapes with plants adapted to growing under very dry or desert-like conditions and inhabited by animals also adapted to these dry conditions. Besides cliff communities of almost pure rock, the most xeric or driest natural community in the Midwest is the desert-like, rocky glade. Many of the plants that grow on prairies also grow on glades, but glade conditions tend to be drier for two main reasons. First, glades lack the deeper soils found on prairies and typically have only thin rocky soils that do not hold much moisture. Second, glades are hotter than prairies because they most often are located on south- and west-facing slopes—strong exposure to the heat and drying effects of the sun.

To reduce water loss, glade plants have evolved to have special characteristics such as small leaves, waxy leaf coverings or hairs on their leaves and stems. Many glade animals tend to be small so they can crawl more easily under rocks for shade. Some glade animals have thick scales covering their skin to minimize evaporation. Other glade animals, such as wolf spiders and kingsnakes, are active when the temperatures are cooler—usually during the morning and night—and take refuge under rocks or in the shade during the heat of the day. Wildlife such as butterflies, grasshoppers and lizards have excellent powers of thermoregulation—they can efficiently heat up and cool down several times during the day.

If you have a dry area on the south or west side of your house in the open sun, you may have problems keeping most plants alive there without constant watering and care. Instead of trying to overcome the hot, dry conditions, establish a small glade community. Consider creating slopes by mounding soil into a softly winding berm about two feet high in the middle. Soil quality is not crucial because most glade plants grow on fairly poor soils. Most glade plants are adapted to well-drained soils, and the sloping sides of the berm help keep an area drainage. Obtain some flat rocks and partially bury one end into the soil on these slopes to provide overhanging shelters for small animals. Place cedar logs on the top of your mounds for fence lizards and other species to use for basking in the sun.

Plant heat-tolerant, short- to medium-height grasses, such as buffalo grass, sideoats grama grass, prairie dropseed and little bluestem, on your glade. Indian paintbrush, lanceleaf coreopsis, rose verbena, yellow puccoon, Missouri primrose, prickly pear cactus and rock pink are all short, but beautiful native grasses and wildflowers adapted to glade conditions. They often attract butterflies and other interesting wildlife. Lists of plants adapted to glade conditions are in Chapter Five.

Dave Tylka

LEFT *By name, glades are a less familiar habitat to many people than forests, wetlands or prairies. But once you visit a glade habitat, you'll soon recognize its dominant features: rocky outcrops, gravelly soil, few trees, and interesting plants and grasses.* **ABOVE** *Five-lined skinks are common on glades; if furnished with enough cover, they can be attracted into your yard if forests are near by. The bright blue tail reveals this one to be an immature male. The blue fades as they become adults.*

larger properties,
more opportunities

Jim Barbort

Chapter Eight

The opportunities for attracting wildlife increase tremendously on larger properties. On most urban or suburban lots, there may be enough room to plant a few large trees or a small patch of prairie. On larger properties, you may have enough space to plant a half-acre or more of prairie, establish or restore forests and create watering holes or landscapes for a wide diversity of wildlife. The guidelines here apply to larger properties of at least one or two acres in size or more.

With several acres of ground, charting sun-shade patterns and concerning yourself about one group of plants shading out another group isn't as crucial as in urban areas because you have the room to spread out your landscapes. The basic steps of planning and designing still apply to larger landscapes, as well as the information for shade and sun landscapes found in Chapters Four and Five.

Larger properties are not limited by cramped spaces, so you can try some of everything. You can add forest and prairie landscapes, create bird and butterfly landscapes in several locations around your house and try to find areas where pool, marsh and glade communities (see Chapter Seven) can be established. On dry sites, consider building or restoring a glade community, adding some of the native plants adapted to dry conditions. On moist sites, you can dig out a depression for a pool or marsh community and use suggestions covered in the quick tips in Chapter Nine for attracting amphibians.

Jim Rathert

What Does the Surrounding Neighborhood Look Like?

Even if you own an acre or two, the best way to see how your property fits into the natural character of the neighborhood is to get an aerial perspective. The larger your property, the more aerial photographs and maps will help you plan. Free aerial photographs are generally available to landowners from the farm service agency office in your county. For a small fee, the office staff may be able to provide you with an enlarged copy of your neighborhood. For even more detail, check into the cost and scale of satellite-generated maps.

To get a better idea of the degree of the slopes on your property and the surrounding land, consult a topographic map. These maps are available for purchase from state geologic survey offices, local offices that deal with public or private land management, or they may be photocopied at public libraries.

If you live in the country or on the outskirts of town, the area surrounding your property may be undeveloped land, retaining much of its natural character. Using maps, determine how far away you are from any good-sized forests or prairies and look for connections or corridors to these natural communities. If the corridor is narrow or non-existent, begin planning for the best opportunities to get connected or enhance existing corridors. Chapter One describes the importance of habitat corridors to wildlife.

CHAPTER COVER PAGE *Deer, turkey and coyotes, among others, are associated with larger, more rural properties, though deer inhabit suburban areas, too.* **ABOVE** *No matter what size your property is, it may be useful to obtain an aerial image of your land and some of the land surrounding it to get an idea of the dominant habitat types.*

Jim Rathert

If a creek or stream runs through your property or if you plan to build a pond, look upstream at the watershed area. If the watershed above you is farmland or developed land, see if a wide riparian area has been maintained. Determine if sediments may be flushed downstream during heavy rains and end up in your pond. If the creek or stream above you flows through a golf course or agricultural lands, you may want to ask the land managers what chemicals they use on their lands or consider testing the water periodically with simple test kits.

Some states have teams of volunteers, such as Missouri's Stream Teams, who monitor water quality and help maintain or restore riparian areas along various stream stretches. Where such a group already exists, consider joining it. If there is not a group working in your vicinity, you may want to start one. If forests and prairies with good riparian areas dominate the upstream watershed, the existing water quality is probably pretty good.

Identify Potential

If you already know where the dry, moist and wet habitats are on your property, you may not have to do much map work. To locate some of the best areas to begin landscaping for wildlife, study photos and maps to find:

  Open areas with potential for sun landscapes, such as prairies

  Open areas or old fields, with potential for establishing or restoring upland or bottomland forests and shade landscapes

  Existing shaded areas or forests with potential for additional ground, shrub or understory layers of vegetation

Jim Rathert

Dry areas on ridge tops or on the drier south- and west-facing slopes that
    are possible glade sites
Moist areas in depressions or ravines as possible sites for pools, ponds,
    marshes or other water features
Locations for small hummingbird and butterfly landscapes

Assess and Inventory Your Property

After coming up with a list of potential areas to landscape, visit these sites
on foot to assess the soil and moisture conditions and inventory the existing
vegetation. If you have doubts about the quality of your soil, contact the county
University Outreach and Extension Service for instructions on collecting soil
samples and getting soils analyzed for a small charge. If you are unsure of the

LEFT *Before wide-spread European settlement, much of the Midwest was
probably dotted with landscapes called savannas—transition areas between
forests and prairies.* **ABOVE** *State conservation or natural resources agencies
often have people on staff to give advice and offer assistance to landowners who
wish to restore or improve their property for wildlife. Agencies often publish guides
that can help with native landscaping projects on both small and larger properties.
Page 173 includes additional sources for native landscaping.*

Jim Rathert

existing composition of the plant communities, get a general idea of what plants dominate your land by using field guides to trees, wildflowers and other plants. For plants that are more difficult to identify, take photographs or collect a 10-inch portion of a tree branch, folding it into a sealed plastic bag to prevent drying, and take it to a nearby nursery or nature center.

Remember that most native trees, shrubs, wildflowers and grasses grow well in nutrient-rich loam soils and, in turn, many plant species have a hard time growing in heavy, clay soils. Native plants that are adapted to clay are noted in the charts found in Chapter Five. On the other hand, clay soils hold water well and make excellent places to locate frog and salamander ponds and marshes. Areas containing shallow, rocky soils, especially when situated on south- and west-facing slopes, drain quickly and make good sites for glade communities.

Soil content and moisture, plus several other factors affect tree growth. Upland hardwood trees, such as oaks and hickories, grow best on well-drained soils on broad ridges or gentle slopes. These upland trees grow larger and produce more acorns or nuts for wildlife on north- and east-facing slopes where soils tend be deeper and richer. Steep slopes, narrow ridges and south- and west-facing slopes support more drought-tolerant trees like the Eastern red cedar and short-leaf pine—both of these are coniferous (cone-bearing) evergreens and furnish excellent wildlife cover.

At the bases of slopes and in ravines, soils tend to accumulate nutrients and retain water—ideal conditions for bottomland, softwood trees such as sycamores, silver maples, willows, river birch and hackberries. Not only do these bottomland trees produce seeds and berries for wildlife, but also their softwoods are ideal for woodpeckers to chisel out homes in. When selecting areas to plant trees, choose

ABOVE *As you begin planning for native landscaping, walk your property and try to imagine it's pre-settlement character. Was it dominated by evergreen trees like these short-leaf pines? Prairies? Wetlands? Combinations of several natural communities?* **RIGHT** *Whether you seek to cultivate wide open spaces or small corners of a yard, using native plants can help you reach your goals and improve over-all biodiversity.*

Cliff White

sites for both upland and bottomland trees. If you have only a few evergreen trees growing on your property, consider planting groves or groupings of Eastern red cedars and short-leaf pine trees.

When selecting potential prairie sites, converting croplands and pastures to prairies is easier than trying to change old fields to prairies because old fields tend to harbor more weed seeds. One of the most important steps for establishing a prairie is site preparation. One or two applications of a contact herbicide on a fescue pasture in the fall, followed by an overseeding directly onto the grass stubble in December, have a fairly good success rate. For seeding prairie areas larger than a half-acre, look into using a special drill and tractor to plant seed mixes of native grasses and wildflowers. If weeds begin to dominate your prairie planting the next year, follow the mowing and burning guidelines described in Chapter Five on page 98.

How Do You Use Your Property?

If your overall goal in landscaping is to attract the widest diversity of native wildlife species to your property by furnishing a variety of wildlife habitats over the long

Jim Rathert

Jim Rathert

term, realize that certain land-use activities may actually reduce biodiversity. Activities such as raising domestic animals for sale or recreation, planting row crops and farming trees will influence a portion of your property's capacity to attract the widest diversity of wildlife. Although short-duration grazing at specific times of the year favors some prairie species over others, long-term domestic livestock grazing on prairie communities reduces the vitality of many plants and the ability to attract wildlife. If livestock graze forest communities, they eat the understory vegetation that normally furnishes food to wildlife. Livestock that get into forests also compact the soil, causing stress to trees.

Planting row crops generally reduces plant and animal biodiversity, except if you grow oil-type sunflowers, white millet or other seeds that are commonly used in bird feeders. These birdfeeder seeds are grown and marketed throughout the midwest because they attract a wide range of wildlife species. If you maximize timber production on parts of your property by removing the less desirable tree species and understory vegetation, this too, reduces the overall wildlife habitat.

If you add only oak trees or spicebushes to your landscape, you only benefit acorn-eating animals such as turkey or spicebush swallowtail butterflies. When you plant only one or two species or manage parts of your property for only one or two types of animals, especially on a large scale, you reduce overall plant diversity, which results in a decrease in wildlife diversity.

Consider the Maintenance

The maintenance guidelines for smaller landscapes described in Chapter Three apply to larger properties as well. The amount of time used to maintain larger areas does increase with size. Larger prairies typically require more time for mowing and conducting prescribed burns. More time is needed to keep longer trails mowed or mulched. If you plant large areas of seedling trees, you need to reduce the surrounding weed growth that competes with the young trees by carefully spraying an herbicide on the weeds or mulching around the base of the seedlings.

Finalize Locations and Select Plants

After visiting the various potential sites for forest and prairie landscapes, finalize the locations and choose which native plants are best suited for each area. Native plants that grow well in the shade or in the sun and attract wildlife are listed in Chapters Four and Five.

Jim Rathert

LEFT *Many shrubs and small trees, such as this flowering dogwood, do well in both shade or sun landscapes and create nice transitions between the two.* **ABOVE** *Count yourself lucky if you have a marsh or wetland on your property. Nationwide, wetland habitats have been cleared and drained on a large scale—to the detriment of great numbers of plant and animal species.*

M. Naumann

Check with your state's conservation or wildlife agency for available native seeds or bare-root plants and trees specifically grown for conservation efforts. Many are available at a minimal price. For example, an excellent source of trees and shrubs for Missouri residents who are planning reforestation, windbreak, erosion control and wildlife habitat projects is through the Missouri Department of Conservation's George O. White State Forest Nursery near Licking, Mo. Most native trees and shrubs for wildlife habitat plantings on larger properties are available in minimum bundles of 25 and special planting assortments for smaller projects. Seedlings are one to three years old and shipped as bare-root plants. Please see page 174 for the nursery address and phone number.

Special Concerns on Larger Properties

If there is a creek or stream running through or along your property, the area of land adjacent to a flowing stream is called the riparian area. These areas are extremely beneficial to wildlife, as well as an important

ABOVE *If you have a stream running through your property, incorporate it into your native landscaping. You can expand the width of its riparian corridor, plant wildflowers on the forest floor, or create a small path leading up to it. The next chapter includes 25 Quick Tips or easy steps you can take to help attract wildlife to your yard.* **RIGHT** *Little bluestem can be considered a staple in sun landscapes.*

place to exercise soil conservation practices. As a general guideline, riparian plant communities should be maintained for 50 to 100 feet back from the banks on each side of the stream to allow for a corridor. Not only do these riparian plants furnish wildlife habitat, but the vegetation also filters rainwater that flows off the surrounding land, stabilizes the stream banks and reduces soil erosion. If this riparian vegetation is lost, sediment and other pollutants wash into the water and cause problems for many fish and wildlife species. Planning efforts should always include conserving riparian vegetation.

In the transitional areas between the forests and the prairies, consider planting the edges or borders with shrubs. A landscape edge is a gradual change in the plant structure, slowly moving from one distinctly different type of vegetation to another. A good edge smoothes out abrupt changes to the landscape and tends to be a winding line and border rather than a sharp square or angular line and edge.

If you decide to plant large patches of prairie grasses and wildflowers, you may want to establish about a 20-foot-wide strip of a non-aggressive, cool-season native grass such as Virginia or Canada wild ryes. This grass strip should be regularly mowed and serves as a future firebreak around your prairie. These cool-season grasses stay green, resist catching on fire and help contain the flames when you use prescribed burns to encourage the growth of native warm-season grasses and wildflowers.

Jim Rathert

quick tips *for* attracting birds, insects *and* herps

Chapter Nine

Growing native plants for wildlife habitat is by far the most important and compelling way to attract wildlife to your property. There are many additional methods to lure wildlife not only to the edges of your property, but also to bring them close to your house so you can observe them. These quick tips are categorized by the wildlife groups they benefit—birds, such as songbirds and hummingbirds; insects, such as butterflies; and herps, which include amphibians, such as frogs and salamanders, and reptiles, such as lizards and snakes.

Birds

1 BASIC AND EFFECTIVE SEED FEEDERS

When putting out the more expensive birdseed, such as black, oil-type sunflower seed, use a clear plastic tube feeder with metal dispensing holes to prevent squirrels from enlarging the holes and destroying the feeders with their teeth. Select a plastic tube feeder that has a replacement tube available. The tubes deteriorate in the sun, while the metal parts last practically forever.

For inexpensive seeds such as millets, construct a simple, wooden platform feeder and scatter the seeds about liberally. Buy a two-foot-long section of a wide (12 to 18 inches), inch-thick, solid wood (not plywood) board to serve as your platform. Nail or screw a strip of narrow trim along the edges to keep the seeds from getting blown or knocked off. Periodically clean the surface of the platform with a weak bleach solution.

2 BEST SEEDS FOR SONGBIRDS

Many factors influence why certain bird species are attracted to one kind of birdseed over others. At its simplest, some birds prefer big seeds and some prefer small seeds. To attract the widest diversity of birds that like big seeds—chickadees, finches and nuthatches—offer black, oil-type sunflower seed in a tube feeder. For birds that prefer small seeds, such as sparrows, mourning doves and buntings, scatter white Proso millet on a platform feeder.

If you live in an open grassland region, you are going to have better luck attracting grassland birds such as sparrows, so increase your millet feeding. In forested regions, you are most likely to attract forest birds, such as chickadees and nuthatches, with sunflower seeds. Most packaged birdseed mixes are selected and marketed to attract people, not necessarily birds, so avoid buying

Jim Rathert

colorful mixes in plastic bags. To get the most for your money, stick to the basic seed types and purchase them in 25- or 50-pound bulk bags.

WHERE TO PLACE BIRD FEEDING STATIONS

3 Bird feeders can be important for bird survival during extended periods of ice or snow cover when natural foods are hard to find. At most other times of the year, the major beneficiaries of bird feeding are probably the birdwatchers. So, for ease of viewing, place feeders where you can see the feeding birds while you're sitting down for a meal or washing dishes. If you place your feeders in view from where you sit and study, read or write, be prepared for major distractions.

For forest birds, you can hang feeders high off the ground for great visibility. Grassland birds, such as sparrows that normally forage near the ground, are best attracted by seeds on a platform positioned close to the ground. Regardless of how high you place your feeder, grow bushes for cover near your feeders so songbirds can escape quickly from predators such as sharp-shinned hawks. Hopper-type feeders obstruct not only your view but may also obstruct a songbird's view of an incoming hawk.

BEST TIME TO FEED SONGBIRDS

4 The best time to feed songbirds is year-round. During warm months, the songbird visitation to your feeding station drops because the birds disperse, set up breeding territories and raise young. If you feed birds only during the winter, you probably miss watching migrants come through your neighborhood, the bright summer plumages of male goldfinches and cardinals, and the unusual behaviors exhibited by young songbirds as they follow their parents around. A widespread myth about feeding birds is that birds become dependent upon your feeder and, if you stop filling your feeder, the songbirds starve. Birds, like most wildlife, are opportunists—if your restaurant is closed, birds will fly elsewhere.

EASY SUET FEEDING

5 In general, suet is any kind of animal fat. Prime bird suet is a special type of solid white, almost flaky animal fat that is found around the internal organs of cattle (especially kidney fat). A suet cake is animal fat mixed with various other foods. Suet mixtures are usually heated and mixed, then poured into shaped forms, onto pine cones or into holes drilled in cedar logs

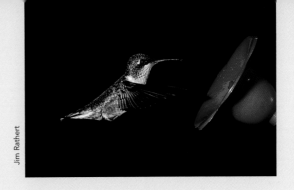

Jim Rathert

and hung up for birds to find. Logs stuffed with suet should be periodically replaced because of bacterial build-up. The attractiveness of suet cakes and mixtures varies according to the ingredients. Some suet cakes can be offered in the warm months, but pure suet is a cool-weather food for Midwestern birds. As the fat breaks down, it smells and becomes unsightly during warm weather.

The easiest way to offer pure suet to birds is in plastic-coated, wire suet baskets or feeders. These are a snap to clean and harbor fewer bacteria. The most convenient size is a rectangular wire feeder about three inches by five inches by seven inches in size, which is easy to fill and readily accommodates downy, red-bellied and even pileated woodpeckers and many songbirds, such as tufted titmice and nuthatches. This high-energy food also attracts other wildlife. You may want to discourage starlings and other undesirable critters from eating your suet by hanging the wire feeder rather than attaching it to a post. Most starlings do not like to swing when they land on a hanging feeder.

For the best and most for your money, purchase bulk amounts (five to 10 pounds) of prime suet from a meat store or processing plant. Spread the suet out on newspapers, cut it up into sizes to fit your wire suet feeder, seal the pieces in plastic sandwich bags and freeze them for later use. Discard suet scraps and newspapers into the trash. Never put animal or dairy products in with your compost.

6 HUMMINGBIRD FEEDING

In addition to wildflowers, shrubs and trees with red, orange and pink tubular flowers, nectar feeders can lure hummingbirds close to your house and encourage them to become neighborhood residents. The best hummingbird feeders are those that do not drip and are the easiest to clean, such as saucer feeders, which hold about 10 ounces of liquid. If small brushes do not come with the feeder, buy some small wire bottle brushes for cleaning the feeder holes and, when bent, for reaching all parts of the reservoir.

Fill feeders with a solution of four parts water to one part sugar. To speed up the process, mark fill lines for the sugar and water with a black magic marker on the outside of a large, plastic cup. To dissolve the sugar, use hot tap water or microwave the water to heat it up. Some people boil the solution to sterilize it. If the hummingbirds empty the feeder every day or two and you clean it well when you refill it, boiling is not necessary.

Do not use artificial sweeteners because they contain no energy. Do not use honey or red food dyes because of health risks to hummingbirds. Even if the birds don't finish off the solution in three or four days, clean and refill the feeder anyway to reduce the risk of disease. If a black fungal growth persistently appears on the feeder, use a weak solution of vinegar or bleach to clean it up. Thoroughly rinse the feeder until the chemical smell is gone, then refill with sugar water.

As with seed feeders, locate hummingbird feeders close to a window where you can enjoy watching hummers come and go. Shady locations are better for hummingbird feeders because the sugar solution breaks down more quickly in the sun. To help hummingbirds find a new feeder, tie a couple of lengths of red ribbon to or near the feeder instead of coloring the water red. Goldfinches and orioles occasionally drink sugar water from saucer hummingbird feeders.

Sugar water not only presents food to birds but also can attract ants. They can best be deterred with a commercially

available, moat-like ant guard that hooks on above the feeder and is filled with water. You can make your own ant guard by drilling a hole in a small plastic cup, inserting an eyebolt and waterproofing it with silicon.

7 YEAR-ROUND WATER

To attract birds and small mammals close to the house, be sure to provide them with water in addition to wildlife food and cover. Year-round water at a bird feeding station attracts birds such as insect-eating wrens and bluebirds that normally do not visit seed bird feeders. Chipmunks, tree squirrels, ground squirrels and even nocturnal flying squirrels may visit your water source.

Bird feeding stores offer a variety of electrically heated devices to keep water from freezing. Although expensive, there is at least one solar-powered, water-heating device on the market. During warmer months, an easy-to-clean water source is a

Jim Rathert

Jim Rathert

glass baking dish about nine inches by five inches by three inches that slips in and out of a wooden frame. Green algae can easily be scrubbed out without soap by using a plastic scrubbing pad. To reduce the chances of disease, periodically use a little bleach when you wash the glass container. Rinse it out again thoroughly.

8 BIRD HOMES FOR CAVITY-NESTERS

Many species of birds and mammals use tree cavities or holes roost and nest in. Woodpeckers commonly drill out natural cavities in standing, upright dead trees—commonly called snags. Fortunately for other wildlife, a woodpecker uses its cavity only once and makes a new one for its next family. Bluebirds, highly beneficial screech owls and flying squirrels commonly use old woodpecker cavities for nests.

Snags in sunny areas can support native vines such as Virginia creeper and yellow honeysuckle. If they do not present a hazard, consider leaving snags around the edge of your yard. If snags are accessible and easily observed from your house, create your own cavities with a portable drill. Be safe; never drill into any snags with over-head branches that could fall.

If you do not have snags around, wooden bird and bat nest boxes provide cavity housing. Information on dimensions, entrance hole sizes and placement are found in publications from your local conservation or wildlife agency office. If raccoons are common in your area and you mount birdhouses on poles, invest in good quality cone-shaped predator guards called baffles. These help prevent nest predation by raccoons, domestic cats and other predators. Hollowed-out gourds have been used for years as purple martin homes and plastic replicas are also available for sale.

For insect-eating birds, such as phoebes and wrens that build nests in nooks and crannies of houses, hang one or two ceramic bird bottles on your house near the corners. Bird bottles are shaped like vases with a slit on the bottom to hang on a nail or screw. Colonial settlers used these to attract nesting birds that would feed on flies and mosquitoes around their houses.

9 WINTER ROOST BOXES FOR BIRDS

Many year-round songbirds use dense vegetation such as red cedar trees for nighttime roosts. When winter temperatures turn frigid, some resident songbirds such as bluebirds gather together in large tree cavities or nest boxes to share body heat. Since spring nest boxes are not designed to conserve heat, consider building a winter roost box or two for communal songbirds. Roost boxes should be sealed with silicon to eliminate airflow and include a series of wooden dowel rod perches inside the box. The entrance hole should be located at the bottom, and the box should face south for solar heat.

10 MEALWORMS FOR INSECT-EATING BIRDS

During cool weather when insects are hard to find, you can give your backyard birds an occasional treat of mealworms. These worms are actually the larvae of darkling beetles (*genus Tenebrio*) that infest granaries and bakeries. Mealworms are available at pet stores or can be purchased from mail-order companies. The easiest way to offer mealworms to the birds is to fill up a

couple of jar lids and set them out on your platform feeder. To keep the lids from tipping over, fasten them to the wood platform with a small tack or screw.

In winter, resident bluebirds and wrens and most seed-eating nuthatches and chickadees will gobble up mealworms. Feedings at spring and fall migrations bring in warblers, vireos and tanagers. When parent birds bring their begging, noisy young to the feeder in spring, take advantage of the great photo opportunity. Mealworms live longer in warm weather if you cool them off in the refrigerator before setting them out for the birds. Include some small pieces of bark for the mealworms to crawl under and avoid the hot sun.

11 FRUIT FOR BIRDS

Supplement fruit-producing shrubs and trees with supermarket fruits to attract resident fruit-eating birds such as mockingbirds, bluebirds and robins. In spring, when most native fruits are not yet available, migrating waxwings, catbirds, orioles and tanagers relish fruits at your feeding station. Scatter raisins and dried

Jim Rathert

cranberries on your platform feeder. For messy treats, such as grapes, grape jelly and sliced oranges, offer these on an old plate or something else that can be removed easily and cleaned. Sugary juices left on platform feeders may encourage bacteria growth, so clean them off with a weak bleach solution and rinse them with water.

12 DUST BATHS

Somewhere in the open sun away from your feeder, create a bird dust bath. If you spend much time outdoors in the summer, you've probably seen birds dusting in a road or path. Birds literally hunker down in a pothole of dust and sand, fluff up their feathers and vibrate their wings in a cloud of dirt. Then, birds go through a preening process using oil from special glands at the base of their tails—the same grooming they go through after a water bath. Dusting is thought to have a therapeutic function associated with feather parasites or molting.

Find a good spot in view of a window, then import some small grain sand and soil or scrape some dry soil into dust. You can frame the dust bathing spot with rocks and logs to blend it into your landscape. Ground birds such as sparrows, quail, doves and turkeys are more likely to do the dust dance.

13 CALCIUM FROM EGGSHELLS

Female birds use calcium stored in their bones to produce hard eggshells that protect their developing young. Crushed chicken eggshells scattered on platform feeders allow female songbirds to replenish lost calcium in the late spring or early summer. To avoid the risk of salmonella food poisoning, first place the broken shell pieces on a small tray in the oven when you bake breads or cakes. Another alternative is to drop large eggshell pieces in boiling water for a minute and crush them after they cool.

14 NEST MATERIALS FOR THE TAKING

As spring weather warms, convert your wire suet basket into a nest material stash for the birds. After a thorough cleaning, stuff the suet basket with small pieces of string, pet hair, cotton balls and feathers. Chickadees, chipping sparrows and wrens use many of these materials in their nests. Tree swallows are particularly fond of using feathers in their nests.

15 SUNFLOWER SEED OPENER

If you watch birds eat sunflower seeds at your feeding station, keep an eye on where the sunflower seed is opened and eaten. Nuthatches, tufted titmice and chickadees often select one sunflower seed from the feeder and fly off to a tree branch to crack it open. When they do this, they wedge the seed into a crevice and peck it open. To encourage birds to spend more time around the feeder, saw several deep grooves into the flat surface of a small length of wood two-by-four. Attach the wood block to a flat surface near your feeder, such as a deck rail. To get them used to using the opener instead of a nearby tree, wedge several sunflower seeds into the grooves when you fill the feeder.

16 BIRD–WINDOW COLLISIONS
Millions of birds fly into windows each year, especially during spring and fall migrations. Birds unfamiliar with the terrain make that all-too-familiar thud against the glass. Many times the birds see a tunnel of light through the house and cannot detect the physical presence of the windowpane. If a bird is only stunned, place a colander over the bird to protect it until it regains its full senses.

To reduce collisions:

Keep window shades pulled on the other side of the room during the day.

Move feeders close to the window to reduce flight speed if birds hit the glass.

Hang some colorful ribbons on the window to signal a barrier.

Hang some netting from an overhang above the window.

Insects

Jim Rathert

17 SUGAR FOR BUTTERFLIES
In the early spring when few plants are flowering, some forest-dwelling butterflies that have overwintered as adults emerge from dormancy. They feed primarily on sugary tree sap and rotting fruit. You can create a similar butterfly sugar mixture by crushing some old bananas and other over-ripe fruit into a mush and combining it with one to two pounds of brown or white sugar and one to two cans of beer. Allow the mixture to ferment in the sun for a few hours in an open container. If you use a jar, remove the lid or just rest it on top to keep

out fruit flies because the gases from fermentation may cause the sealed jar to explode.

To attract question mark, comma and mourning cloak butterflies to a sugar station, pour or apply the sugary mixture to tree trunks with a spatula to look like oozing tree sap. Or, if the solution smells bad, pour it into a wide, flat container that can be composted later.

Bees, ants and some other interesting insects may visit the mixture for a sugary meal. If underwing moths are in the neighborhood, they will visit the mixture soon after nightfall. The best way to observe moths at night is by flashlight with a piece of red cellophane covering the beam. During the day, underwing moths rest on tree trunks where their gray forewings are camouflage and cover the colorful hindwings of red, yellow and orange.

18 SAND FLATS FOR ANT LIONS

Ant lions are among the most fascinating insects in the Midwest. They can be attracted to your property by spreading out a flat layer of sand on the ground about three or four inches deep over an area about four to six square feet. In the wild, ant lions seem to prefer sheltered areas under a rock overhang. Consider locating your sand flats in a sheltered area such as under an overhang of your house.

Dave Tyika

The ant lion larvae construct small, unusual volcano-shaped pits in the sand about two or three inches in diameter where they prey on ants.

Although ant lion larvae are only a half-inch long, their jaws make up more than 50 percent of their body size. Mostly buried in the sand, they wait motionless at the bottom of the volcano until an ant falls into the pit. Because of the slope, the ant slides right down to the bottom and into the jaws of the ant lion. Beneficial sand and digger wasps may also nest in the sand flats. These solitary wasps are not aggressive toward humans.

19 WET GROUND FOR PUDDLING BUTTERFLIES

Consider creating a small depression a few feet around and filling it with wet sand or mud for butterflies. On a smaller scale, a container of sandy soil can be buried in a low spot of the yard. Male swallowtail, sulphur and blue butterflies commonly congregate at similar areas in the wild and siphon up primarily sodium in a process called puddling. Males apparently need more sodium than females. Small amounts of salt can be added to the sand, but remember that salt is toxic to many plants. Male butterflies are also attracted to sodium and nitrogen dissolved in the soil at old campfire sites and pools where mammals have urinated. To replicate these conditions, sprinkle the remains of charcoal briquettes on moist soil.

20 OVERWINTERING BUTTERFLIES

Overwintering butterfly houses are marketed in many garden centers and magazines. Presumably, these houses accommodate butterflies such as question marks, commas and mourning cloaks that overwinter as adults. Although the houses are decorative, their actual use by butter-

Jim Rathert

flies is highly questionable. In nature, these butterflies overwinter in caves, rock crevices, thick tree bark and brush piles.

21 HOLLOW STICKS FOR SOLITARY BEES AND WASPS

Social bees and wasps tend to guard their nests aggressively and sting humans and other mammals who get too close. Solitary bees and wasps, on the other hand, have stingers but seldom use them against large mammals or humans. They are not

Jim Rathert

aggressive insects. Many solitary bees and wasps—and even a few social bees and wasps—are important predators of insects and spiders. One beneficial group of solitary wasps, called mud daubers, sting spiders and collect them to provision their mud nests. Inside the mud nests, the wasp eggs hatch into worm-like larvae and feed on the living, but paralyzed spiders.

To create homes for solitary bees and wasps, attach hollow sticks, such as sumac stems or blackberry canes (with the pith removed), to horizontal shrub and tree branches with a twist wire from a bread wrapper. You can tie several stems together with stovepipe wire and attach them to branches or horizontally secure them on fencing, rock walls or any surface a few inches from the ground. Seal or leave solid one end of the hollow stems.

Small blocks of a pine or cedar two-by-four with partially drilled holes can also be attached or hung horizontally as wasp and bee homes. To keep them from getting too hot in the sun, locate the wooden blocks near trees for partial shade.

LEARN ABOUT PESTICIDES

According to the National Audubon Society, about 70 million pounds of synthetic pesticides are applied annually around the home—that's about eight pounds per U.S. citizen. Native landscaping reduces the need to control pests with pesticides because biodiverse areas tend to keep pests in control naturally. Before spraying the area around your home with any synthetic pesticides, learn about the health risks posed by these chemicals and investigate if any less-toxic, natural substitutes are available. For guides on home pesticide use, contact www.audubon.org/bird/pesticides/index.html or www.epa.gov/pesticides. Other groups to contact include the National Pesticides Telecommunication Network (www.ace.orst.edu/info/nptn/index.html) and the National Coalition Against Misuse of Pesticides (www.beyondpesticides.org/)

Jim Rathert

Amphibians and Reptiles

22 TOAD CELLARS

Toads do not give or cure warts, but they are especially active at night and eat large quantities of insects. Some toads actively search for prey while others hang around brightly lit areas and patiently wait for flying insects to come to the light, then fall to the ground. Although not strictly nocturnal, toads retreat to a cool refuge during the day.

To protect and encourage toads, you can create daytime toad shelters. Around the informal edges of your yard, dig a hole about a foot square and cover the bottom with a few inches of sand. Then dig a three-foot-long, gently sloping trench from the hole up to the surface and lay a three-inch-

169

wide plastic pipe in the trench. Stacking rocks on top of each other in the hole, create cavities near the end of the pipe large enough to house a good-sized toad. Throw some soil back over the top of the rocks, cover up the plastic pipes, and you've just built a toad cellar.

These cellars may be used by other herps, such as salamanders and small snakes, and even a chipmunk or rabbit, depending on the diameter of the plastic pipe. If you are curious about what uses the cellar, substitute the rock shelter with a bottomless, wooden box and a removable lid. Nail together four one-foot lengths of old one-by-six boards into a square frame. Bury your frame six inches deep and cut out a one-foot-square board to rest on top and cover the frame. Run your pipe out under the wooden frame. Attach a handle to the lid so you can easily lift it off the frame, carefully and quietly look inside and then replace it.

23 LOG REFUGES FOR SMALL HERPS

Flat pieces of slab wood from sawmills can be scattered throughout informal gardens in your yard and even in flowerbeds to serve as hideaways for red-backed and slimy salamanders. Ground skinks, fence lizards and small snakes, such as ring-necked, midland brown and worm snakes, take advantage of these refuges. If a sawmill is not nearby, use round logs that have been split or sawn in half length-wise to create one long, flat surface. On the flat surface, saw some different-sized grooves to serve as tunnels for salamanders under the flat surface of the log.

Place the logs flat side down. Because ideal conditions vary for different herp species, place some in the sun and some in the shade to vary temperature and moisture conditions. Usage will change according to the season and the time of the day. If you check periodically under the logs for wildlife, always lift up the edge away from you so fleeing animals have an avenue of escape away from your feet.

24 BASKING SITES FOR LIZARDS

Fence lizards and skinks are common insect-eating lizards in the Midwest. To elevate their body temperatures and metabolisms high enough in the morning to catch insects, they must bask in the sun. Cedar logs and rocks elevated a foot or two above the ground serve as excellent basking sites. In breeding season when the male fence lizard's throat turns blue and the male five-lined skink's throat turns orange, these perches also serve as places from which they establish and stake out their territories. In addition to color

Jim Rathert

displays, male fence lizards bob their heads up and down and perform push-ups to threaten territorial intruders.

25 FISHLESS PONDS AND SALAMANDERS

If your house is nestled in a forested area with shallow depressions on the land, you may want to create a salamander pond. Dig out about two feet of soil from these low spots and try to set aside an area of at least 10 square feet. Avoid building steep banks; gradual slopes are better. Spring and fall breeding forest salamanders each need water about five continuous months during the year, while toads need only two months of water to breed. Small frogs need three months.

Small, temporary fishless ponds create breeding sites for several beautiful mole salamander species. Spotted and small-mouthed salamanders use the ponds in spring while ringed and marbled salamanders may use these ponds in the fall. For successful breeding, male and female salamanders need small twigs and tree branches in the water. Leave these branches in place each summer when the water gets low or dries up. Males attach spermatophores—packets of sperm—to these dry branches and, during courtship, receptive females will pick up the sperm and lay fertilized eggs a few days later.

Sources

BROCHURES FROM THE MISSOURI DEPARTMENT OF CONSERVATION

(Many other state conservation agencies produce similar publications)
Single copies available free

Backyard Bird Feeding

Butterfly Gardening and Conservation

Enjoying Missouri's Birds

Lizards of Missouri

Missouri Toads and Frogs

Missouri's Oaks and Hickories

Missouri Conservation Trees and Shrubs

Planning and Conducting Prescribed Burns in Missouri

Ruby-throated Hummingbirds in Missouri

Snakes of Missouri

Wildflower Favorites

BOOKS

The Amphibians and Reptiles of Missouri (Second Edition). Tom R. Johnson. 2000. Missouri Department of Conservation, Jefferson City, MO. 400 pp.

The Audubon Society Handbook for Butterfly Watchers, A Guide to Observing, Locating, Identifying, Studying, and Photographing Butterflies. Robert Michael Pyle. 1984. Charles Scribner's Sons, New York. 274 pp.

The Backyard Naturalist. Craig Tufts. 1993. National Wildlife Federation, Vienna, VA. 79 pp.

Building a Backyard Bird Habitat. Scott Shalaway. 2000. Stackpole Books, Mechanicsburg, PA. 116 pp.

Butterflies and Moths of Missouri. J. Richard and Joan E. Heitzman. 1996. Missouri Department of Conservation, Jefferson City, MO. 385 pp.

Butterfly Gardening, Creating Summer Magic in Your Garden. Created by the Xerces Society in association with the Smithsonian Institution. Sierra Club Books, San Francisco. 192 pp.

Going Native, Biodiversity in Our Own Backyards. Janet Marinelli Editor. 1996. Brooklyn Botanic Garden, Brooklyn, NY. 112 pp.

Go Native, Gardening with Native Plants and Wildflowers in the Lower Midwest. Carolyn Harstad. 1999. Indiana University Press, Bloomington, IN. 278 pp.

Landscaping for Wildlife and Water Quality. Carrol Henderson et.al. Minnesota Department of Natural Resources, St. Paul. 175 pp.

Landscaping with Native Trees, The Northeast, Midwest, Midsouth & Southeast Edition. Guy Sternberg and Jim Wilson. 1995. Chapter Publishing, Shelburne, Vermont. 288 pp.

Landscaping with Wildflowers, An Environmental Approach to Gardening. Jim Wilson. 1992. Houghton Mifflin, Boston. 244 pp.

Missouri Wildflowers (Fifth Edition). Edgar Denison. 1998. Missouri Department of Conservation, Jefferson City, MO. 276 pp.

A Natural History of Trees of Eastern and Central North America. Donald C. Peattie. 1977. Houghton Mifflin Co., Boston. 606 pp.

Ozark Wildflowers, A Field Guide to Common Ozark Wildflowers. Don Kurz. 1999. Falcon Publishing, Inc., Helena, MT. 262 pp.

Seasonal Guide to the Natural Year, A Month by Month Guide to Natural Events in Illinois, Missouri and Arkansas. Barbara Perry Lawton. 1994. Fulcrum Publishing, Golden, CO. 328 pp.

Shrubs and Woody Vines of Missouri. Don Kurz. 1997. Missouri Department of Conservation, Jefferson City, MO. 387 pp.

Spring Wildflowers of Missouri State Parks. Bruce Schuette. 1991. Missouri Department of Natural Resources, Jefferson City, MO. 91 pp.

Walking with Wildflowers, A Field Guide to the St. Louis Area. Karen S. Haller. 1994. University of Missouri Press, Columbia, MO. 257 pp.

NATIVE PLANT NURSERIES IN THE LOWER MIDWEST

(For a current list of Grow Native! retail nurseries, go to www.conservation.state.mo.us/ programs/grownative)

ARBOR VILLAGE
P.O. Box 227
Holt MO 64048
816/264-3911

BLUEBIRD NURSERY INC.
P.O. Box 460
Clarkson NE 68629
402/892-3457

BLUESTEM PRAIRIE NURSERY
13197 E. 13th Road
Hillsboro IL 62049
217/532-6344
email: bluestem@cillnet.com

CASCADE FORESTRY NURSERY
22033 Fillmore Road
Cascade IA 52035
391/852-3042
email: cascade@netins.net

DABNEY NURSERY
5576 Hacks Cross Road
Memphis TN 38125
901/755-4037

EARTH MIRRORS NATIVE WILDFLOWERS
5643 Sunnywood Drive
Cedar Hill MO 63016
636/274-2951

ELIXIR FARM BOTANICAL
County Road 158
Brixey MO 65618
417/261-2393

ENDERS GREENHOUSE
104 Enders Drive
Cherry Valley IL 61016
815/332-5255
email: endrsnatvs@aol.com

FORREST KEELING NURSERY
88 Forrest Keeling Lane
Elsberry MO 63343
800/356-2401

GEORGE O. WHITE STATE FOREST NURSERY
Missouri Department of Conservation
14027 Shafer Road
Licking MO 65542
573/674-3229

GILBERG PERENNIAL FARMS
2906 Ossenfort Road
Wildwood MO 63038
636/458-2033

H. E. NURSERY
R.R. 3, Box 4
Litchfield IL 62056
217/324-6191

HAMILTON SEEDS & WILDFLOWERS
HCR 9, Box 138
Elk Creek MO 65464
417/967-2190

HOLLAND WILDFLOWER FARM
P.O. Box 328
Elkins AR 72727
800/648-3737

ION EXCHANGE
1878 Old Mission Drive
Harpers Ferry IA 52146
800/291-2143
email: hbright@means.net

J & J SEED LLC
29341 210 Street
Gallatin MO 64640
660/663-3165

LAFAYETTE HOME NURSERY
R.R. 1, Box 1-A
Lafayette IL 61449
309/995-3311

LONGVIEW GARDENS, INC.
11801 E. Bannister Road
Kansas City MO 64138
816/765-5664
email: winyardlongview@aol.com

MCGINNIS TREE & SEED
309 E. Florence
Glenwood IA 51534
712/527-4308
email: qrun@awol.com

MISSOURI WILDFLOWERS NURSERY
9814 Pleasant Hill Road
Jefferson City MO 65109
573/496-3492
email: mowldflrs@sockets.net

NATIVE GARDENS
5737 Fisher Lane
Greenback TN 37742
865/856-0220
email: sales@nativegardens.com

THE NATURAL GARDEN
38W443 Highway 64
St. Charles IL 60175
708/584-0150

NOLIN RIVER NUT TREE NURSERY
797 Port Wooden Road
Upton KY 42784
270/369-8551
email: nolinriver@hotmail.com

P. E. ALLEN FARM SUPPLY
R.R. 2, Box 8
Bristow NE 68719
402/583-9924

PAN'S GARDEN
Star Rt. Box 70-C
Mountain View MO 65548
417/934-6537

PECASUGAR NURSERY
13002 Harrison Road, P.O. Box 22
Shirland IL 61079
815/629-2546

PINE RIDGE GARDENS
832 Sycamore Road
London AR 72847
501/293-4359
email: pineridg@cswret.com

RICHARD CLINEBELL
3820 Hartford Street
St. Louis MO 63116
314/772-9151

RIDGECREST NURSERY
3347 Highway 64
Wynne AR 72396
870/238-3763
email: ridgecrest@crosscountybank.com

ROCK POST WILDFLOWER NURSERY
5798 Windy Meadows Lane
Fulton MO 65251
573/642-6927
email: mikeann@sockets.net

SHARP BROTHERS SEED CO., MISSOURI
396 SW Davis St. - Ladue
Clinton MO 64735
660/885-7551
email: sharpbro@iland.net

SHARP BROTHERS SEED CO.
P.O. Box 140
Healy KS 67850
316/398-2231

SHAW NATURE RESERVE
P.O. Box 38, Highways 100 & I-44
Gray Summit MO 63039
636/451-3512
email: scott.woodbury@mobot.org

SHOOTING STAR NURSERY
444 Bates Road
Frankfort KY 40601
502/223-1679

STOCK SEED FARMS, INC.
28008 Mill Road
Murdock NE 68407
800/759-1520
email: stockseed@alltel.net

SUNLIGHT GARDENS
174 Golden Lane
Andersonville TN 37705
865/494-8237
email: sungardens@aol.com

TREES BY TOULIATOS
2020 Brooks Road
Memphis TN 38116
901/345-7361

WALKER'S GREEN SPACE
2699 53rd Street
Vinton IA 52349
800/837-3873

Index